M000023409

The Real Woman

Grows Roses from the Thorns of Life

Joyce Tilney

Unless otherwise indicated, all Scripture quotations are taken from the *New King James Version* of the Bible.*Holy Bible: New Kings James Version*® (NKJV).Copyright © 1983 by Thomas Nelson, Inc. Used by permission of Thomas Nelson Publisher. All rights reserved. *New King James Version, Holy Bible*, copyright © 1982. *New King James Version New Testament and New Testament, with Psalms*, copyright © 1980, 1979.

All Scriptures marked NIV are taken from the *Holy Bible, New International Version*®, NIV®. Copyright © 1973, 1978, 1984, 2011 by Biblica, Inc.®. Used by permission. All rights reserved worldwide. (All niv Scriptures taken from the previous 1984 copyright are distinguished by including "1984" beside the Scripture reference. Published by International Bible Society. Used by permission of Zondervan Publishing House. All rights reserved.)

All Scriptures marked NLT are taken from the *Holy Bible, New Living Translation*. Copyright © 1996, 2004, 2015 by Tyndale House Foundation. Used by permission of Tyndale House Publishers, Inc., Carol Stream, Illinois 60188. All rights reserved. (All NLT Scriptures taken from the 1997 copyright are distinguished by including "1997" beside the Scripture reference. This earlier edition is titled *Praise and Worship Study Bible*, copyright © 1997 by Tyndale House Publishers, Inc.., Wheaton, Illinois 60189. All rights reserved.)

All Scriptures marked *The Message* or MSG are taken from *The Message*. Copyright © 1993, 1994, 1995, 1996, 2000, 2001, 2002 by Eugene H. Peterson.

The Scripture marked TLB is taken from *The Living Bible*. Copyright © 1971 by Tyndale House Foundation. Used by permission of Tyndale House Publishers, Inc., Carol Stream, Illinois 60188. All rights reserved.The Scriptures marked AMP are taken from *The Amplified Bible, New Testament*. Copyright © 1958, 1987 by The Lockman Foundation, La Habra, California.

The Scriptures marked KJV are taken from the *King James Version* of the Bible.

The Scripture quotation marked TPT is taken from *The Passion Translation of the Bible, Broadstreet Publishing Group, 2015.*

Copyright © 2018 Joyce Tilney, Women of God Ministries, Inc.
All rights reserved.

ISBN: 978-692-05295-2

Cover Design: wendywalters.com
Book Interior: endlesspress.org

Contact: therealwomanjt@yahoo.com
https://www.facebook.com/WomenofGodMinistries/
www.wogministries.com
www.whydiets.com

No part of this publication may be reproduced, stored in a retrieval system, or transmitted in any form, or by any means electronic, mechanical, photocopying or otherwise without the prior written consent of the author, Joyce Tilney.

Endorsements

Joyce Tilney has tapped into a deep vein of hope and truth in her book, The Real Woman. In a world where people are depressed and pessimistic, this book is like a ray of light in the darkness pointing to a joyful and overcoming life. *I love it!*

Cindy Jacobs
Generals International

Joyce Tilney's book, "The Real Woman Grows Roses From the Thorns of Life," is a rousing and encouraging book, to women and men alike, about the divine ability of God to make us stronger and better despite and even because of our challenges, when we hold onto His Word above all else.

Joyce powerfully reminds women that they have been redeemed and invited by Jesus, to choose the better part, which is intimate relationship with Him - restoring their significance and strengthening their character.

"The Real Woman Grows Roses From the Thorns of Life" is a firm dose of truth, empowering women and men to know that in each other they have been given by God a strong partner in advancing the Kingdom of God.

Dr. Ché Ahn
President, Harvest International Ministry
Founding Pastor, HROCK Church, Pasadena, CA
International Chancellor, Wagner University

Rev. Joyce and Pastor Bill Tilney have been dear friends for decades, and beloved ministerial associates with us in southeastern Pennsylvania for a number of years where we pastored. The book you are holding is a must read! It is both powerful and practical! Once again, Joyce wields the pen of a ready writer as in all her books. (Ps. 45:1)

This one is no exception! Being 'real' means being authentic. Joyce shows us authentically how to be who we are in Christ. In an 'unreal' world, it is crucial that we find our true identity and destiny in God's word. While this book is obviously directed to women specifically, it has broad application to one and all. Be prepared to be mighty blessed.

Rev. Robert P. Garret, M.Div.
Founder/President Christian Call Bible Institute
www.robertgarrett.org

With so many voices in today's culture telling women how to think and act, Joyce Tilney has written a timeless book where page after page is filled with life lessons from the Word of God and from her personal life experiences.

Our identity as women can only be found in who God says we are, created in His image, filled with purpose and vision. The Real Woman takes us on a journey to the heart of God and gives us points to ponder as we give our hearts to Him. I believe the Holy Spirit will bring revelations for healing, renewal and restoration into women's lives as they read this book and discover truth for daily living.

Pastor Erma Zimmerman
Petra Church, Hopewell Network of Churches
New Holland, PA

A few years ago, I had the honor of meeting Joyce Tilney at a conference. The blessings from that divine opportunity have continued to unfold. I began attending her monthly Women of God Ministries' meetings in the greater Philadelphia area. Joyce provided rich, inspired teachings, designed an opportunity for fellowship and created an atmosphere where women were inspired by her real life stories combined with biblical truths. She met a need for authentic women's ministry.

In her latest book, "The Real Woman," Joyce once again provides ministry to women in her unique style using her strengths I've come to know and love. Her knowledge of the Word and ways of God are woven together with stories of real women of the bible. Joyce provides the added dimension of sharing her real life experiences of faith, life, and growth as a woman of God in an authentic, sometimes humorous and always purposeful manner. Read this book. Your life will be enriched. You'll be inspired. You'll feel like you've been with a wise woman who truly knows God and authentically desires for you to know Him, too. You'll be challenged to grow in your knowledge of God, His Word, and His Ways. Finally, you'll believe that you, too, can become the real woman He created you to be!

Nancy L. Miller
Certified Life Coach & RN
Navigate Life Coaching, LLC
Greater Philadelphia Area, PA

Dedication

To the beautiful women of God in my life. You are truly
'Real Women,' and I am so blessed to call you family!

My daughter, Jen Tilney Allen and her twin daughters,
Kayla and Heather.

My daughter-in-love, Lindsay Graber Tilney and her
daughter Jessica.

My daughter-in-love, Lisa Tilney Tucker and her
daughter Samantha.

You bless my life every day as I watch you grow into
becoming the Women God has created you to be!

Acknowledgments

To my best friend, husband and lifelong partner, Bill.

Did we have any idea of the twists and turns that our lives together would take? Thank you for making each turn smooth and secure even in the darkest hours when there seemed no way out.

I appreciate your faith in our God and always trusting Him for all of our needs. For your godly example in leading our family to a life of peace and joy in the God we serve. Thank you for giving me the freedom to develop the gift that God has imparted within my spirit. I love you and value your friendship.

My friend in the Lord, Marilyn Price, editor.

You have encouraged me in your walk with the Lord, and I appreciate your gift in helping authors share their heart with the world. Thank you for 'fine-tuning' my writing and helping to make it clear and simple, so that others can run and not faint in the day of adversity.

A friend in the Lord is a Joy to the heart

Some of my most powerful words from the Lord have come as I shared with my friends in the Lord. Just what we think of as "casual conversation," over a good cup of tea (or coffee),

God speaks! One thing I picked up while living in Scotland was sharing a good cup of tea with friends. I'm still a tea lady!

When I was teaching a seminar, during lunch time I was having a conversation with a dear woman of God, Kay Behle. She said to me, "Joyce, don't you have a book, *The Real Woman*?" I said, "No," but at that moment the Holy Spirit sparked within me the desire, and an outline was downloaded for *The Real Woman*. I went home and told my husband about the plans for my next book, *The Real Woman*.

Always have an open heart to hear the Lord. He has no set pattern, and I can tell you when you are trying to hear, you won't because your mind is involved. God speaks to your spirit when you are relaxed and enjoying life.

I have been blessed with strong women of faith during my life who have very quietly, unknowingly shared words of wisdom. Barbara Crockett, Carol Stroble, Kay Kern and Helen Kurtz are four of those women. Their faithfulness to God and their servant hearts made a big difference in my life. They served at Women of God Ministries in Pennsylvania cleaning the room, making food and praying for me, always faithful and dependable.

LaVeta Warner, longtime friend and board member for Women of God Ministries, served us while we were living in Scotland. taking care of stateside business. Most of all, she is a friend in the Lord, accepting me even on my bad hair days!

Contents

"We can complain because rosebushes have thorns, or rejoice because thorn bushes have roses."

Abraham Lincoln

Foreword

In *The Real Woman*, Joyce Tilney has written a landmark book which will serve as a reference book for every serious Christian woman who desires to grow and produce fruits of good living in their lives to God's glory.

I am persuaded not only women but men will benefit tremendously from reading this book as well. As I have read this amazing book I find on every page, eternal truths and principles which God has provided for every Christian in His Word. These principles are there to enable us to navigate the vicissitudes and trials of this life and to triumph over the various challenges in the power and authority of the Spirit of the living God. In every chapter of this book you will find interspersed words of wisdom that are in the category of wise sayings that I am reaching for my highlighter to note and memorize them so that they can stand me in good stead as I seek to walk the path that God has designated for me to follow.

This book is destined to be a bestseller for Christians who intend to maximise every opportunity to discover the gifts and treasures God has made available to them to make their way prosperous and victorious. In my opinion, it should be recommended reading for every serious minded disciple of Jesus Christ who intends to do exploits for God and live on "Victory Lane"

As usual Joyce Tilney has written in a most clear and readable manner. In her usual very encouraging way Joyce has presented the truth of the Word of God in such a way that it is accessible to everyone, no matter where they are at in their walk with God. As an adroit Teacher of the Word and indefatigable Coach who sees potential and possibility in everyone, she presents the solutions and pathways that God has provided for Christians to walk victoriously and make the most of every situation, even difficult ones, in order to show the goodness of God in their lives and to turn the situations around to His glory, à *la* Rom 8:28.

As you read this book a hunger will be created in you to know the Lord more, to walk closely with Him, to receive fresh revelation and to follow the direction that He has chosen for you.

Joyce Tilney has carefully crafted this book "The Real Woman" for every Christian woman (and man) to navigate the challenges of life fully leaning on the Word of God and His directives in a way to ensure you can peacefully walk in the perfect will of God.

Joyce presents so very clearly the need for daily prayers, reading the Word of God regularly and walking in the Spirit that you cannot read this book and remain the same.

If you want to learn how to keep your peace in the face of life's daily disappointments and challenges and live victoriously at the same time, this is the book for you.

It will wake up your spiritual life and show you how to develop intimacy with God.

Joyce has presented a rare insight as to the challenges faced by the saints of old compared to our present day experiences and how the principles of the victories they obtained can be ours today. Her wealth of experience in the ministry and years of walking by the Word permeate every page and enriched the book.

Citing examples of women in the Bible who experienced challenges to what the average woman experiences today, Joyce shows powerfully how through the application of the principles provided in the Word of God they were able to obtain victory and do exploits. Thus today, by applying the same principles we can similarly, also experience the power of God in our lives as part of our daily experience.

This is not a book to read and walk away from. This is a book that will change your life for good. At the end of each chapter there are points to consider and as you meditate on these you will find your whole outlook being transformed as you align yourself with the Word of God and yield to the leading of the Holy Spirit.

Get ready to be challenged, encouraged, motivated and promoted to new levels of living in the supernatural power and grace of God! Here comes the glory!

Rev. Kemi Ajayi
Apostolic Team, Kensington Temple
London, England

She Shall Be Called Woman

Long before God formed woman's physical body, you were in His heart and mind.

"Then God said, 'Let Us make man in Our image, according to Our likeness; let them have dominion over the fish of the sea, over the birds of the air, and over the cattle, over all the earth and over every creeping thing that creeps on the earth.' So God created man in His own image; in the image of God He created him; male and female He created them. Then God blessed them, and God said to them, 'Be fruitful and multiply; fill the earth and subdue it; have dominion over the fish of the sea, over the birds of the air, and over every living thing that moves on the earth.' " (Genesis 1:26-28)

It is very important that you understand the beginning of mankind. You, woman of God, are not an afterthought! You were in His heart and mind before you were created! "Let US make man (mankind), *let them, male and female* have dominion, He blessed *them*, and said to *them*, 'Be fruitful and multiply; fill the earth and subdue it; have dominion....'" That is your mandate in life, and you are responsible to honor God in the image He has made you to be – woman. It is very clear here that male and female have dominion, and they are both to be fruitful and multiply.

Women have graced this earth with insight, sensitivity and beauty, spiritually and physically. We need to note that Eve entered the physical world as an equal, not in a dominant or a subservient role. It was God who said, "It is not good that man should be alone; I will make him a helper comparable to him" (Genesis 2:18). God took the rib of man and formed woman, and He brought her to the man. Adam had nothing to do with her creation other than taking a nap.

Within the equality of their creation, there are distinct differences in their role and function.. A woman should never settle for being treated as anything less than what she was created to be – a woman created in the image of God. It is our responsibility to grow in our identity and uniqueness as a woman created in His image.

Abraham Lincoln, a man of great wisdom, stated: "Nothing stamped with the Divine image and likeness was sent in the world to be trodden on."

In God's creation He set the boundaries, but He placed within man and woman a free will, the ability to make choices. Our life is constructed by the choices we make, good and bad. God honors our decisions, even if they go against Him. This is evident in the Garden. Eve had a choice to make, and she had to live with the consequence of her choices. From the day that Adam and Eve took a bite of the forbidden fruit, there has been tension between man and woman.

"Where are you?" was the first question God asked (Genesis 3:9). "Where are you in your relationship with Me?" They had enjoyed relationship and fellowship, but now He has to confront their sin and explain the consequences of that sin.

The serpent, woman and man were all judged that day. God's judgment of the serpent foreshadowed events to come. Satan clearly understood that his demise would come through woman the day the Savior of the world would be born of a woman. It is the devil himself who has the destruction of woman in his plan.

In the Jewish culture, women were not treated much better than their Roman and Greek sisters. We know that God did use women in the Old Testament with great influence and we will study their lives later. But in general, women were considered a commodity.

In the culture that Jesus was born into, women were treated with no value or appreciation. They were devalued, defiled and degraded; and unfortunately religion played right into the hand of the enemy. Women were not permitted to learn, to speak to men in public, even their own husbands. A Pharisee began his day by thanking God that He had not made him a Gentile, a woman or a slave! This was the world that Jesus, our Savior, walked into!

When Jesus said, "...Mary has chosen that good part..." (Luke 10:42), it got the attention of everyone around. Jesus shook the foundation of society with those words! Everyone thought Jesus would tell Mary to leave. But clearly this was an invitation for women to come and dine, eat from the words of the Lord.

Jesus came to destroy the works of the devil (1 John 3:8) and to restore God's original design for men and women and their purpose in this world. When Jesus saw women crushed and hidden behind closed doors, He flung the doors wide open!

He took these abused female image bearers and put them center stage to play leading roles in God's redemptive plan for the world.

Jesus made the way for mankind, including women. John 1:11-12 tells us, "He came to His own, and His own did not receive Him. But as many as received Him, to them He gave the right to become children of God, to those who believe in His name."

The 'Real Woman' is the woman who receives Jesus Christ as her Lord and Savior. She understands the work of redemption and reflects the love of God in her life. She wears her robe of righteousness and garment of praise with dignity. When she walks into a room, everyone knows that there is something different about this woman and they are attracted to her presence.

As they watch her life, they are amazed with the grace and strength with which she encounters the trials of life. Yes, walking the runway of life has many challenges, but the Real Woman, born again by the Spirit of God, faces each day trusting in her Lord, because she was born to overcome. First John 5:4 tells us, "For whatever is born of God overcomes the world. And this is the victory that has overcome the world – our faith." The Real Woman grows roses from the thorns of life.

Walking in the light while living in a dark world is not an easy assignment, but as we grow in the grace and knowledge of God's Word, confident in our identity as a Woman of God, we will follow His footsteps as the Holy Spirit leads us by the still waters.

The Real Woman understands the battles of life are not against flesh and blood, but are against principalities, against powers, against the rulers of darkness that try to kill, steal and destroy her life and the lives of her family. (See Ephesians 6:12).

The Real Woman understands that we have been given everything pertaining to life and godliness through the knowledge of God's Word. Only the Holy Spirit, our Helper, can reveal the promises of God to us that trample on the powers of darkness. We have total access to the Kingdom of God through Jesus Christ.

Life has many unplanned detours, making it very hard to dodge all the thorns of life. You learn to take the fertilizer – the hurts, heartaches and disappointments of life – and grow roses!

God told us in Romans 15:4 (TPT), "Whatever was written beforehand is meant to instruct us in how to live. The Scriptures impart to us encouragement and inspiration so that we can live in hope and endure all things."

One thing we need in this world is hope.

As we read the testimonies in the Bible, we can find strength and comfort as we understand God's great love and His faithfulness to His people. When you read the Bible, don't read with a casual attitude like these are just stories to read to your kids. These are testimonies to teach us and give us understanding in the ways of the Lord, to establish our faith in God that all things are possible with Him! He is your rock and your anchor in time of trouble.

As you read this book, you will laugh and you will cry as you understand your significance as a woman of God and your place in society. Stand tall, woman of God, and walk straight with your head held high because you were created for great work in the Kingdom of our God.

My mother's legacy to me was a love for God's Word. I pray that as you read this book, this love for God's Word will be imparted to you and you will pass that on to the generations that follow you!

> *"She is clothed with strength and*
> *dignity, and she laughs without fear of*
> *the future."*
> *Proverbs 31:25* NLT

*A Rose speaks of love silently in
language known only to the heart.*

Chapter 1

Becoming the Real Woman

*"The wise woman builds her house,
but with her own hands the foolish one tears hers down"*
Proverbs 14:1 <small>NIV</small>

Living in Scotland, one thing I loved was the beautiful gardens. I could look out my windows and see the foothills of the Highlands. I had often told my daughter, "Most people only see this on a postcard, but God has given us a firsthand look at the beauty of His creation in Scotland."

My favorite flower was the rose. I was blessed with this beautiful flower in my own garden. I loved watching the seasons of the rosebush. It was a very sturdy bush, and it could withstand the storms and adverse conditions of its life.

In the spring season I would watch for the little buds forming and growing out from this ugly little thorn bush. Then the color of the flower would start peeking through, and one day the rose burst through! The thorn bush had been changed into a beautiful rosebush! New life had come. God, Your creation is a wonder!

I was enjoying the beauty of the roses in my garden one morning, looking at the delicate petals and enjoying the rich fragrance that came forth when my husband walked up, and I said, "Look at these beautiful roses." He stopped, looked where I was gazing, and said, "What about the thorns?" "Thorns," I cried. "How can you think about thorns looking at this beautiful rose?" His answer, "Thorns are always there; roses bloom in season."

As I was pondering these words, the Lord spoke quietly in my spirit: "The Real Woman grows roses from the thorns of life." I knew that the Lord had a message in this, and I began to study the seasons of a rosebush, or depending how you look at it, the thorn bush.

As I studied the season and growth cycle of the rose, I began to understand what the Lord was showing me. The Real Woman, a woman who is born again, a new creation in Christ Jesus, must grow into this new life in Christ.

Whether we come to Jesus as a young child or after we have walked through a lot of the world's dirt, we must be cleansed. The blood of Jesus cleanses us from sin, but the dirt we pick up in this world must be removed by the cleansing of the washing of water by the Word of God. (See Ephesians 5:26; 1 John 1:7).

The biggest challenge in becoming the Real Woman is unwrapping the real you! Becoming the Real Woman is an inside job, a work of the Holy Spirit within. "For it is God who works in you to will and to act in order to fulfill his good purpose" (Philippians 2:13 NIV).

*The biggest challenge in becoming the
Real Woman is unwrapping the real you!*

The most important transition in your life is forming a godly character. Character is what sustains you when the only thing you can do is stand when you are waiting on the Lord. When you feel alone and that no one loves you, your best friend, the Holy Spirit, will whisper in your ear, "You are the beloved and you are accepted." Hope springs forth and the bud begins to grow from the thorns, the hurts and the heartaches of life, to bring a new season as life begins to flow!

As little girls we played make-believe, loving to dress up and dream of being the perfect woman, wife and mother! We start early in life to compare ourselves with others and develop a competitive attitude.

We must not buy into the world's image of a successful woman – Suzy homemaker one day and the self-sufficient woman the next day; one day a dependent weakling and the next an independent woman juggling all the plates in the air and working out all the problems of the world!

When we have become a victim of false identity, we hide and cover up the real woman whom God created. Damaged women learn to survive living in regrets of the past or fantasizing about the future.

We live in a false world. We have false teeth, hair color, false nails and push-up bras, but we can be real in a false world.

Most people describe themselves by their roles and duties. "I am a wife," or "I'm a teacher," whatever they are doing in life. This sets us up for a life of confusion because roles in life are constantly changing. *Life isn't about what we do, but it's about who we are.* Who you are has an impact on what you do and how you do it. I have many different roles in life. I am a wife, a mother and a friend, among many other roles. But in my own life I am always playing the lead role, and it is always opening night! Many women live as though they are performing a written role, directed by people around them who are judging their performance.

The good news is that we are new creations in Christ Jesus, and God says it is okay to be yourself. Our job in life is to find and unveil the woman He created us to be!

We are not expected to do this by our self; He has given us a Helper, the Holy Spirit, who will lead us into all truth. God revealed Himself to us by taking on the form of a human in Jesus Christ. He is asking that we do the same in revealing ourselves to Him in response. As we open our heart and soul to Him, allowing the truth to set us free, we will find the freedom, security and peace we desperately need living in this world.

Life is a process. In the process we find the promise. In the process we find the provision. In the process we find the purpose. When you find purpose, you find the presence of God in your life. Living in His presence is the door to the supernatural power of God where "all" things are possible to him who believes (Mark 9:23).

Our first priority is to maintain a personal relationship with our Father. Devotion to His Word and an ongoing awareness of His presence in our daily walk give us stability, confidence and keeps us in step as we pursue the path that He has chosen for us.

Time is our most valuable asset. We all have the same amount of time: 60 seconds in a minute. We have been given the responsibility to choose how we use our time and value the time given to us on this earth.

Time is the measure of life, and the quality of our life is determined by how we use our time. God created time for man, but God doesn't live in time.

> *Time is the measure of life, and the*
> *quality of our life is determined by how*
> *we use our time*

"To everything *there is* a season, a time for every purpose under heaven" (Ecclesiastes 3:1). Our time is in His hands. We must learn to walk in the rhythm He has set for our life.

As a woman of God, a consistent lifestyle of reading the Word, meditating on the Scriptures and prayer will keep you in a place where you can hear His voice and be led by the Holy Spirit. You don't have to read the whole Bible in one day. Investing a small amount of time over time brings increase in things that matter most!

What matters most? Jesus said, "But one thing is needed, and Mary has chosen that good part, which will not be taken away from her" (Luke 10:42). Like Mary, we must choose the good part.

Today's technology makes it easy and convenient to hear the Word. Driving your kids around, on your way to work, exercising, or doing housework all give you the opportunity to put the earphones in and be blessed as you go through the routine of your life. Get to work early, sit in the car ten minutes and focus your mind on God by reading a verse for the day. Over time this little ten-minute habit will make a big difference in your life.

As we study the women in the Bible, married and single, we see strong women of faith who inspired others, influenced nations and changed the culture of their day.

Jochebed intervened on behalf of her son, Moses, who led the children of Israel out of bondage in Egypt. She also raised two other leaders, Miriam and Aaron. This mother changed her world and set the stage for the deliverance of her nation from her home while on her knees.

Esther was instrumental in the King's Court in saving her nation. An orphan girl, who could have allowed bitterness to harden her heart towards God, chose to be used by God for her people.

Rahab, a prostitute, was instrumental in Israel's victory over Jericho.

Mary carried the seed of God's Son in her womb – a young woman chosen by God for the supernatural birth of His Son. Under Mary's care He grew and became strong in spirit, filled with wisdom.

Lydia, being a respected businesswoman, opened the door for Paul to share the gospel in Europe.

God has always used women who were surrendered to His will for their lives. They all had problems in their lives and in their families. If you want to study the life of a dysfunctional family, look at Abraham, Isaac and Jacob. Somehow God worked through all the lies, favoritism and deceit to build the house of Israel.

Leah is one of my very favorite women in the Bible. She was a substitute bride, rejected by her husband, betrayed by her father and hated by her sister. How do we get the idea that as a woman of God, we are never going to have any more problems? The good thing, as a woman of God, is that you have a Helper, the Holy Spirit, to walk you through all the challenges that you will ever face.

And then there is the Proverbs 31 woman. At one time in my life, I said, "God, I'm not going to another women's conference and listen about this perfect woman. Where did she come from? She is just too good to be true!" She was a strong, intelligent, resourceful woman. She used her skills in a personal business; she dressed herself attractively and helped the poor. Now don't stop reading. Just like you, she was not the perfect woman, but she was a woman who understood the seasons of her life and knew how to prioritize her time not only for her life but also for the life of her family and her work.

She didn't try to do everything herself. She was not afraid to ask for help. God did not design any one person to carry her burden alone. Trying to do it all by yourself does not win you brownie points with anyone including your husband or mother-in-law! It is the road to burnout which many times leads to bitterness.

We find the secret of the Proverbs 31 woman in verse 30: "Charm is deceitful and beauty is passing, but a woman who fears the LORD, she shall be praised."

"Fear," as used in this verse, means reverence; a divine trust in God that only comes by relationship.

Her reverence and respect for God and His Word set her

apart from the world. She did not seek to please others by the decisions she made. She did not seek the opinion of others for acceptance or a sense of value.

"Reverence" is an attitude of your heart which determines the thoughts, words and actions in your life .She looked to God for guidance in every area of her life. Yes, shopping by the Spirit finds the best bargains in town!

> *Reverence is an attitude of your heart*
> *which determines the thoughts, words*
> *and actions in your life.*

When we take a good look at the characteristics of this woman, we see that her life was not that different than ours. She respected her husband. She fed and clothed her children. She used her skills daily. She kept her personal appearance pleasing and was kind to others. Basically, she did the best she could with what she had.

We don't need to feel that what she attained is out of reach for us today. It is allowing God to help us in our daily responsibilities. When we humble ourselves and ask God for help, He is more than able; He is willing. Two of the keys that unlock the door to your purpose in life are humbly acknowledging your dependence on God and accepting His ways even when it takes you out of your comfort zone. I can guarantee this will happen. I was lying in bed crying after we first moved to Scotland. It was cold, it was dark and dreary and I had never lived in a city. I cried out, "Lord, I didn't sign up for this!" He kindly spoke, "You said, YES!" I learned to be content, just like the Apostle Paul!

Do you remember the widow in 2 Kings 4:1-7? She was in a desperate state. Her husband had died and left so much debt that her creditors were coming to take her two sons! She went to Elisha, the man of God, and asked for help.

I think she was expecting a check, not his question, "What do you have in the house?" But she suddenly remembered, "Nothing in the house but a jar of oil." His directions were even more outlandish than his question! How was a "little" jar of oil going to make a difference in her life? Believe me, when God is involved, we can see that it makes a big difference! "Go, borrow vessels from everywhere, from all your neighbors – empty vessels; do not gather just a few. And when you have come in, you shall shut the door behind you and your sons; then pour it into all those vessels, and set aside the full ones."

Can you imagine going to your neighbors asking for empty vessels? I'm sure most of them knew her situation. As she went down the street, don't you know the neighbors were watching and talking? "She's that woman always down at the church giving her money away. Now she has nothing!" She was happy to shut the door when she came home.

We have to be willing to look foolish in the eyes of the world! What a time she and her sons had as they rejoiced in the faithfulness of their God! Remember, obedience is the key. Job 36:11 tells us, "If they obey and serve Him, they shall spend their days in prosperity, and their years in pleasures. "I don't know what the oil was worth, but she paid all the debts and lived on the rest. This is the God we serve "who is able to do exceedingly abundantly above all that we ask or think, according to the power that works in us" (Ephesians 3:20).

As a woman of God you are not limited to this world. You serve a supernatural God who turns your little into abundance! (John 10:10).

As you read and study the lives of the women who have walked before us, you will be encouraged and strengthened in your walk with God. He is the same yesterday, today and forever! (Hebrews 13:8).

So, I ask you, woman of God, what is in your house? Nothing, but the oil of the Holy Spirit whom the Father has sent to help you in your time of need.

Last, but not least, don't forget to take time to smell the roses! Life is a gift to enjoy, not a problem to solve. There is nothing better than having fellowship with your brothers and sisters in the Lord or having a quiet time with your cup of tea, and studying the Word of God.

Family time is the best! Enjoy your time with family, building precious memories that bring strength and encouragement to your soul. Have some "girl time"! It is in these times when you are relaxed that God can speak to you and lead you through the struggles of life.

Remember, ignorance is what the enemy uses to steal, kill and destroy in your life. Hosea tells us in 4:6, "My people are destroyed for lack of knowledge...." That is why Paul tells us in 2 Timothy 2:15, "Study to shew thyself approved unto God, a workman that needeth not to be ashamed, rightly dividing the word of truth" (KJV).

If you fear the thorns, you will never
pick the roses.

Points to Ponder:

- Life is a process.
- Time is your most valuable asset.
- You are born to overcome as a child of God.
- You have a Helper.
- Cultivate a godly character.
- Pursue excellence in all things.
- Live intentionally.

Chapter 2

It's Your Time in the Garden

"Redeeming the time, because the days are evil."
Ephesians 5:16

When you are born again, you step into the Garden of your life. Conversion gives you the ability to "see," and you understand that just like Eve you were created in the imagie of God. You were created to serve God in this earth. Psalm 115:16 tells us, "The heaven, *even* the heavens, *are* the Lord's; but the earth He has given to the children of men."

In the Garden God blessed mankind and told them to be fruitful, multiply and take dominion (Genesis 1:28). This command still stands today. The day of your salvation opened the door for the divine plan devised just for you as you enter a new relationship with God for all eternity. Psalm 139 tells us that we were designed in intricate detail and that our days were ordered before we were ever born. Many people just settle for salvation (which is good!), but do not realize there is a divine purpose for them in this earth as they walk through the Garden of their life. You have been endowed with gifts and skills for Kingdom purposes.

God loves to orchestrate people, places and things in our pathway to lead us to the places and purpose for our lives.

As we begin our walk with God, we need to look at Eve's life. She had the perfect home, the perfect husband; everything seemed to be going her way! As I was pondering this thought one day, I said, "God what happened?" the Holy Spirit whispered in my ear, "She did not value the Word of God."

Eve did not value the Word of God

Second Corinthians 11:3 tells us, "But I fear, lest somehow, as the serpent deceived Eve by his craftiness, so your minds may be corrupted from the simplicity that is in Christ."

Satan's only weapon in the Garden was deception. It is the same today, and Paul is warning us how easy it is to be deceived in this world.

Eve knew God's Word regarding the tree, but in the end, she valued the serpent's word over God's Word; therefore she was deceived.

As women of God we are called to "be diligent to present yourself approved to God, a worker who does not need to be ashamed, rightly dividing the word of truth" (2 Timothy 2:15).

The Word of God is life to those who find it and health to their bodies. Proverbs 4:20-22 tells us, "My son (and daughter), give attention to my words; incline your ear to my sayings. Do not let them depart from your eyes; keep them in the midst of your heart; for they are life to those who find them, and health to all their flesh." This is a foundational scripture – a scripture that you build your life on!

You must be consistent and diligent in the Word of God. How did Jesus defeat the enemy? "It is written..." (Luke 4:4). To defeat the enemy in your life, you must do what Jesus did!

When the Word of God is hidden in your heart, it will come forth from your mouth in times of temptation and trouble.

When you value the Word of God and the truths that are hidden in the Word for you, you will have the spiritual weapons you need to defeat your enemy who has one goal in your life: to steal, kill and destroy your divine purpose. He knows you are a threat to him; you know who he is and how to defeat him. The Word of God is an offensive weapon. In Ephesians 6 where Paul is telling us about the armor of God, verse 17 tells us, "Take the helmet of salvation, and the sword of the Spirit, which is the Word of God."

The sword of the Spirit, the Word of God, is the only thing empowered by the Holy Spirit that can stop the enemy from destroying your life. I don't dwell on the enemy. I value the Word of God and dwell in His Word so I can be sensitive and alert to the enemy's deception.

Every time you open the Word of God and meditate His Word, you are fighting the good fight of faith and defeating the enemy from stealing from you. *This is spiritual warfare!*

The revelation of God's Word in our heart will show us the weapons of warfare and how to fight. The Holy Spirit, our Helper will lead us into the battle releasing the weapons to stop the fiery darts of the enemy.

As we walk through the garden of our life, we need to understand there are seasons of life in the natural and in the Spirit.

The God who has ordered seasons – winter, spring, summer and fall for the earth to bring forth its harvest – has also ordered seasons in our spiritual life to bring forth our maturity, growth and harvest in His "due season." There is a purpose for each season, and if we don't discern the season we are in, we can dig up our seeds and prolong the manifestation of God's promises in our life.

Each season has its own uniqueness. Wintertime has the shortest days, limited sunlight, a time we want to stay inside and hibernate. In the winter we can be cold and complain about it, or we can make some necessary adjustment and be comfortable. We must do the same in the Spirit.

Wintertime is a time to ponder those things told to you by the Lord and plan for spring. It's a time of reflection and adjustments. We often feel like we are having a wilderness experience. God is not hearing you or speaking. Winter is a time when God strengthens your root system, getting rid of the old and preparing for the future. It is extremely important that during the winter we keep our eyes on Him and listen carefully for His voice so He can reveal the mysteries of the Kingdom of God.

In this season of growth we learn lessons of life and obedience that bring stability and confidence which enable us to prepare and receive the harvest. We will all walk through many private victories in our daily routine of life preparing us for our purpose and destiny in the Kingdom of God. Private victories come from small acts of obedience to the voice of God. The voice of God is the place of rest where we can enjoy His presence as we plan for the future. Embrace the winter and look expectantly for springtime.

Springtime is all about embracing new life, new beginnings and preparing the ground for new seeds. As the sun shines on the earth, we feel new desires to fulfill the purpose of God in our life. We walk with confidence and assurance that the God in heaven is with us and has promised to never leave us or forsake us.

As we enter the summer, we prepare our self for long days of hard work. It is time to pull weeds and water the soil of our heart.

Summer is a time when we learn to balance our life of work and play. We must take the time for rest and refreshment and learn to fellowship with our sisters and brothers in the Lord.

We step into the fall season with anticipation of the harvest. As we have been diligent in the other seasons, we know that we will be rewarded with an abundance of God's blessings. Fall is a season of thanksgiving and celebration as we see the faithfulness of God rewarding our diligence. You realize that in the midst of trials and tribulation you have kept your faith in God and received your reward.

"But without faith *it is* impossible to please *Him*, for he who comes to God must believe that He is, and *that* He is a rewarder of those who diligently seek Him" (Hebrews 11:6).

We must understand that satan is the god of this world (2 Corinthians 4:4), and as we live in this world, satan is always trying to deceive us and destroy us. As we mature in the Word of God, it gets easier for us to discern the seasons and walk through them.

We must have fellowship with like believers, people who have the same desire for God's Kingdom that we do. You can draw strength from one another during the good times and the bad.

Nothing we are going through is new to God or man. Solomon tells us there is nothing new under the sun. Everything has a time and a season and the more time we spend in His Word and in His presence, the more we grow in the knowledge of God. His strength is made perfect in our weakness (2 Corinthians 12:9).

Just remember, there is a divine purpose for your life, and it is bigger than you are. The road will not always be easy, but God has promised He will never leave you or forsake you. As you walk the runway of life, you will hear His voice saying, "'This is the way, walk in it,' whenever you turn to the right hand or whenever you turn to the left" (Isaiah 30:21).

> *Just remember, there is a divine purpose for your life, and it is bigger than you are.*

Remember to value the Word of God. It is life to those who find it and health to their flesh! We must learn to be content, not complacent.

In this ever-changing world, God is looking for women of God who are strong and confident in their uniqueness as women created in His image to influence the world they live in.

This is your time in the garden of life and your responsibility to redeem the time that was stolen in the Garden.

*"For I know the thoughts that I think toward
you, says the LORD, thoughts of peace and
not of evil, to give you a future and a hope".
Jeremiah 29:11*

Points to Ponder:

- We must value the Word.
- The Word is life to those who find it.
- The Word in your heart is the foundation of your faith.
- Reading the Word is spiritual warfare.
- God rewards diligence.
- Understand the seasons of life in the natural and spirit.
- You have a purpose in life.

Your heart is a garden, your thoughts are seeds,
You can grow flowers or you can grow weeds.

Chapter 3

Preparation of the Heart

*"Above all else, guard your heart, for everything you
do flows from it."*
Proverbs 4:23 NIV

Life flows from the heart in the natural and in the spiritual.
The Message Translation says, "Keep vigilant watch over your
heart; that's where life starts."

God designed a remarkable pump, and placed it in man's
chest. It is called the heart. There is no machine on earth that
works as hard as the human heart. Reading articles on the
Internet, I found that on average, a healthy heart weighs 11
ounces and pumps 2,000 gallons of blood through 60,000 miles
of blood vessels each day! A healthy heart allows you to enjoy
the life that God has given you.

On the other hand, an unhealthy heart causes disease in
our bodies which brings pain and suffering. Our activities are
limited in our daily lives as much time has to be given to care
for the needs of the body. An unhealthy heart leads to death
– the death of dreams, visions and the purpose God has put in

your spirit, which is also known as your spiritual heart. Your spiritual heart is the center core of your body, which is the temple of the Holy Spirit when you are born again.

When you are born again, you receive a new heart. We are told in Ezekiel 11:19-20, "And I will give them singleness of heart and put a new spirit within them. I will take away their stony heart and give them a tender, responsive heart, so they will obey my decrees and regulations. Then they will truly be my people, and I will be their God" (NLT).

God made man an intellectual, moral and physical earth creature with spiritual responsibility and integrity. Man was created to express God's own nature of love, to receive His love and share His love. Man did not evolve or arrive on earth by accident; he is fearfully and wonderfully made for a purpose (See Psalm 139).

According to *Vine's Expository Dictionary,* the "heart" stands for the inner being of man, the man himself. It is the fountain from which life springs forth. "He also taught me, and said to me: 'Let your heart retain my words; keep my commands, and live'" (Proverbs 4:4). So we must understand how important our heart and the Word of God are connected to work together to bring life. Throughout the Word of God we are reminded of the connection between our words and our heart. "Let the words of my mouth and the meditation of my heart be acceptable in Your sight, O Lord, my strength and my Redeemer" (Psalm 19:14).

What's in your heart affects everything you do! Is your heart full of bitterness, hate, jealousy or unforgiveness? A healthy physical heart comes from a healthy spiritual heart.

Lack of care for our physical heart comes from a lack of care of our spiritual heart. *That is the heart of the matter!*

The truth is that you have received everything from God you are ever going to receive from Him in your spirit, your spiritual heart, when you are born again. You received a Helper, the Holy Spirit (John 16:7). First John 2:20 says, "But you have an anointing from the Holy One, and you know all things." The Holy Spirit who is within you knows all things. The Christian life isn't about "getting" from God; it is a process of learning to release what you have already received in your spirit into your mind. We call this process renewing our mind (Romans 12:2). Philippians 2:12-13 tells us, "Work out your own salvation with fear and trembling, for it is God who works in you both to will and to do for His good pleasure." As women of God, we live from the inside out!

The Holy Spirit, our Helper, teacher, and comforter, dwells within us and is always present to reveal the truth of God's Word to us so that we can comprehend the Scriptures and become on the outside what we possess on the inside! Our physical body will reflect what is in our spiritual heart.

"The spirit of a man will sustain him in sickness, but who can bear a broken spirit (heart)?" (Proverbs 18:14). "Whoever has no rule over his own spirit (heart) is like a city broken down, without walls" (Proverbs 25:28). A city without walls has no protection against attacks of the enemy. You do have an enemy and he has one goal: to steal, kill and destroy. You, as a child of God, have a big God and He has given to you all things that pertain to life and godliness.

The challenge in life is to keep a healthy spiritual heart which will produce good fruit. In studying the parable of the sower, Jesus lets us know just how important it is to understand the condition of your heart.

After teaching to a great multitude about the parable of the sower, His disciples came to Him asking about this parable. In Mark 4:13, He said to them, "Do you not understand this parable? How then will you understand all the parables?" This verse should burn in your heart! If you don't get this, how will you understand anything else!

This parable is about the Sower, the Seed and the Soil. You are the sower. You have the responsibility to sow the seed of God's Word into your heart. I urge you to study this parable in each of the gospels: Matthew 13, Mark 4, Luke 8 and glean from all three. Luke says very clearly, "The seed is the word of God" (Luke 8:11).

The soil of your heart is the only variable in this parable. The sower and the seed always remain the same. Preparation of the soil of your heart will determine how you receive the seed. As the seed sown in your heart is revealed to you by the Holy Spirit, you are going to have a heart change.

You must continue in the Word of God daily to understand your privileges as a child of God. John 1:11-12 tells us, "He came to His own, and His own did not receive Him. But as many as received Him, to them He gave the right to become children of God, to those who believe in His name." You have a right as a child of God to know and understand the principles that govern the Kingdom of Heaven.

We know that the will of God is, "Your kingdom come. Your will be done on earth as it is in heaven" (Matthew 6:10). This is fulfilled as we, the children of God, learn His ways from the Scriptures and walk in them as we walk the runway of life.

As we read and meditate the Word of God, we must ask the Holy Spirit to give us a spirit of wisdom and revelation of the knowledge of His Word. When we receive revelation, then we "see" the Kingdom of God. Ephesians 1:15-23 is another scripture passage that we must understand to be able to prepare the soil of our heart and establish a firm foundation so that we can stand against the attacks of the enemy.

It is only by the help of the Holy Spirit that we can keep the soil of our heart nourished and cultivated to receive the seed of God's Word. John 16:7 tells us, "Nevertheless I tell you the truth. It is to your advantage that I go away; for if I do not go away, the Helper will not come to you; but if I depart, I will send Him to you."

God knows that you cannot live in this world and enjoy your benefits of the Kingdom of God without the help of the Holy Spirit. Are you taking advantage of your advantage over this world? All you have to do is ask!

Near the end of His time on earth, Jesus gave the disciples what I call the ultimate promotion. " No longer do I call you servants, for a servant does not know what his master is doing; but I have called you friends, for all things that I heard from My Father I have made known to you" (John 15:15).

Jesus had brought the disciples into the heart of the Father. In friendship we discover what pleases Him and we respond to His love and walk in the desire of His heart. A servant doesn't know what the master is doing and works for approval and attention.

As we grow in the Word, He entrusts us with more of His power and we are naturally changed into His likeness. As we become confident in our identity as a child of God, we will not be crippled by the opinions of others. We will not work to "fit in" with other people's expectations, but we will burn with the desire to please the Father. We will learn to be content and willing to wait upon the Father for His perfect will for our life.

Mary and Martha are excellent examples to show us the difference between servants and friends.

"Now it happened as they went that He entered a certain village; and a certain woman named Martha welcomed Him into her house. And she had a sister called Mary, who also sat at Jesus' feet and heard His word. But Martha was distracted with much serving, and she approached Him and said, 'Lord, do You not care that my sister has left me to serve alone? Therefore tell her to help me.' And Jesus answered and said to her, 'Martha, Martha, you are worried and troubled about many things. But one thing is needed, and Mary has chosen that good part, which will not be taken away from her'"(Luke 10:38-42).

There are several things that stand out to me about these scriptures. Jesus knew Martha and Mary. He purposely entered a "certain" village for a "certain woman." There was much more to this visit than just a casual gathering. Jesus understood the wide gulf between men and women when He entered this world. He came to set the captives free! Women had been kept in bondage and captivity by religion long enough. This was the beginning of a new day for women. They also received the promotion, no longer a servant but a friend.

Martha had not received the revelation of this promotion, but Mary got it! She was totally at ease when she sat down in the midst of the men to listen to Jesus' words. Sitting at His feet, a hunger was birthed in her heart. Her purpose in life became clear; a conviction began to grow within her.

Martha also knew Jesus and was comfortable with giving Him a piece of her mind! When Jesus spoke, "But one thing is needed, and Mary has chosen that good part, which will not be taken away from her" (vs. 42), it was an invitation for Martha and all women to come and receive from the table that had been set before them. That invitation still stands today!

This is the most liberating statement for women throughout the ages. We must choose and Jesus clearly tells us what is needed and what to choose – the good part, which will not be taken away!

Mary sought to please Jesus by being with Him. Martha sought to please Him through service. Martha is making a sandwich that Jesus didn't order, and Mary discerned the time and season of the day.

This is revealed in more detail in Mark 14:1-9. Mary poured costly oil on Jesus' feet and was highly criticized. Jesus not only defended her, but He praised her. "She has done what she could. She has come beforehand to anoint My body for burial" (vs. 8). Mary discerned the time and season. As she focused and meditated on His Word, she developed spiritual insight and understanding.

"Assuredly, I say to you, wherever this gospel is preached in the whole world, what this woman has done will also be told as a memorial to her" (vs. 9). The fragrance of her obedience still permeates through society today! We are still talking about her. Mary was a woman with insight who chose the good part.

We will only have the freedom that Mary had as we do what she did. She sat at His feet and opened her heart to receive His Word. She meditated on the Word, and the Holy Spirit opened her eyes to understand the time and season of life.

> *We will only have the freedom that*
> *Mary had as we do what she did.*

The next time we hear about Mary and Martha is at the death of their brother recorded in John 11:1-44. When their brother became sick, they sent word to their friend, Jesus. After two days Jesus went to meet with Mary and Martha. Before Jesus got to them, Lazarus had died and was buried.

When Martha heard that He was coming, she charged out to meet Him, saying, "Lord, if You had been here, my brother would not have died" (vs. 21). Jesus explains to Martha that He is the resurrection and asks her if she believes. "Yes," she answered and walked away (vs. 27). Martha confronted Jesus in an accusing manner for not coming sooner.

When she returned, she told Mary that Jesus had come. Mary ran out to meet Jesus and fell at His feet, saying to Him, "Lord, if You had been here, my brother would not have died" (v. 32).

The same words Martha had spoken, but a different response from Jesus! Jesus wept and asked where they had laid Lazarus. Mary did not understand the delay in Jesus coming to them, but it did not affect her relationship with Him. She fell at His feet in worship sharing the sorrow of her heart.

As they walk toward the grave, Martha speaks up again! "He stinks!" (See v. 39). I'm sure Jesus gave her the look and said, "Did I not say to you that if you would believe you would see the glory of God?" (v. 40). When Lazarus walked out of the grave Martha finally got it!

As Jesus looked on, I believe there was a smile on His face that a certain woman in a certain village had finally understood her friendship and received her promotion.

Like Mary, we must make a choice to choose the good part and abide in God's Word. As we feed our hearts, our heart will feed our mouth in our time of need. What was the difference between Mary and Martha? They both spoke the same words, but got different results. Mary's heart was tender towards the Lord, Martha had a hard heart.

Mary had prepared the soil of her heart to receive the seed of God's Word, giving her wisdom and understanding with insight into the times and season of the day.

Martha had been too busy to prepare her heart by meditating God's Word. She had knowledge, but no revelation of the Word to give her understanding and insight.

Your words will bring life or death in every situation that you face in this world. Proverbs 18:21 tells us, "Death and life *are* in the power of the tongue." "You are snared by the words of your mouth; you are taken by the words of your mouth" (Proverbs 6:2).

Your words have power. You were born again by the words that you spoke! "For with the heart one believes unto righteousness, and with the mouth confession is made unto salvation" (Romans 10:10). You were translated from the power of darkness into the Kingdom of light by the power of your own words! That is awesome!

We must understand how important our words are. Isaiah 57:19 tells us, "I create the fruit of the lips...." We can clearly see in the testimonies of Martha and Mary the power of our words. What determines the response to our words? The condition of the soil of our heart.

Many people are living in bondage in a garden thriving with thorns and thistles deeply rooted in their life simply because of fear, pride and spiritual blindness. The Holy Spirit will till the soil of your heart so you can receive the truth of the Word. He will soften areas of hardness and break down resistance and unbelief, but you have to cultivate a heart that is receptive to the seed of God's Word. Your most valuable acreage is the soil of your heart!

Good seed will not grow in bad soil, no matter how hard you toil.

Points to Ponder:

- *Life flows from the heart.*
- *Above all else guard your heart.*
- *Your heart must be cultivated to receive the seed planted.*
- *You have been promoted from servant to friend.*
- *Words bring life or death.*
- *God creates the fruit of your lips.*

Chapter 4

Plant Your Own Garden

"The seed is the word of God"
Luke 8:11

Many women search for the "Real Me" only to be deceived and disappointed. They compare themselves with others and the worldview of the perfect woman, never being able to reach this unobtainable goal.

Some women are looking for the dream man who will make them happy. Mothers live their lives through their children, and when they leave home they feel useless and empty.

There is no man on earth who can meet all of a woman's needs. Women and men were designed to complement each other and to work together in their unique gifts and callings.

True womanhood cannot be measured by a man's love or the praises of society. There is only one standard and one source of power that is able to withstand the challenges of life and the constant changes in the world – the Word of God.

A woman of God has the power within her to overcome any-thing she faces in this world. She understands that she has total access to the Kingdom of Heaven and that she is not limited to the world she lives in.

Too many Christian women have forsaken the empowerment God has implanted within them. They fall into the trap of satan and rely on outsiders to meet their needs.

There is no other person, male or female, who can fulfill the task of making us content or complete. Our happiness and satisfaction do not come from our position in life, our status or a spouse. We must take the responsibility of cultivating our own heart and learn to take the fertilizer, the hurts and heartaches of life, and grow roses from the thorns of life.

After a while...

*After a while you learn the subtle difference between
holding a hand and chaining a soul and you learn that
love doesn't mean leaning and company doesn't
always mean security.
And you begin to learn that kisses aren't contracts and
presents aren't promises and you begin to accept your
defeats with your head up and your eyes ahead with the grace
of a woman, not the grief of a child
and you learn to build all your roads on today because
tomorrow's ground is too uncertain for plans and futures
have a way of falling down in mid-flight.
After a while you learn that even sunshine burns if you
get too much, so you plant your own garden and
decorate your own soul instead of waiting for
someone to bring you flowers.*

And you learn that you really can endure, you really are strong and you really do have worth and you learn and you learn with every good-bye you learn.

Veronica A. Shoffstall

You alone are responsible for your heart. Fellowship with other sisters and brothers in the Lord is valuable and gives you encouragement and help along the path, but only you can plant seeds in your garden. Attending church, hearing the Word and sitting under the anointing of the Holy Spirit are also vital to watering your garden.

Your heart is God's Garden just waiting to flourish. It is time to pick up your garden tools and pull some weeds and plant some seeds! As we prepare to plant some seeds, we need to understand the importance of the seeds in our heart. We read in Genesis 8:22, "While the earth remains, *seedtime and harvest*, cold and heat, winter and summer, and day and night shall not cease."

Everything God does in our life starts with a seed. This is an eternal pattern of life. Seeds are planted; they grow until harvest comes, and then this cycle is repeated. Cold and heat are two extreme conditions facing all seeds planted. Summer and winter represent seasons in our life. Day and night, dark and light, are the daily cycles of renewal.

Everything God does in our life starts with a seed.

49

As a woman of God, it is a new day, a new season for you. A time to plant new seeds and reap new produce in your life.

When Jesus spoke to the disciples about the Kingdom principle of the seed, it was not something new. The seed principle had been in place from the beginning. Jesus identified it and then explained it to the disciples and for generations to come.

Jesus taught in parables to protect the truth hidden in the Word from those who choose not to believe Him. When people desire to hear, understand and perceive Kingdom principles, He responds to them with healing, forgiveness and insight.

I mentioned the parable of the sower before, but it is so important I feel we need to look further into it. As mentioned before, this is a key parable in the Word as Jesus taught it as the key that unlocks other parables. "Do you not understand this parable? How then will you understand all the parables?" (Mark 4:13). There is power in understanding this truth!

Luke very clearly tells us that "the seed is the word of God" (Luke 8:11). We must understand the importance of this statement as this is the door to understanding everything. The Word of God is the seed that makes His Kingdom work in our lives. We must be Word possessed! Meditate on it continually (Joshua 1:8), asking the Holy Spirit to open the eyes of our understanding. This is a simple but profound truth: The seed is the Word of God.

The parable of the sower tells us the enemy will try to steal our seed, to choke it and destroy it, but when it is firmly rooted in our heart it will stop the fiery darts of the enemy! The Word of God that is in your heart is the foundation of your faith.

We must be intentional about what we plant, because our

harvest comes from those seeds. If you are not happy and satisfied with your life, then you need to take inventory about the seeds that you have planted. There is a seed for everything you need in the Word of God.

> *We must be intentional about what we plant, because our harvest comes from those seeds.*

Why does this work? Because "you have been born again, not of perishable seed, but of imperishable, through the living and enduring word of God" (1 Peter 1:23 NIV). The Word is incorruptible seed, and every seed contains life in itself!

One day I noticed that signs of spring were beginning to be seen, and I opened my door. Much to my surprise, a purple petunia was in full bloom growing from a crack in the brick patio. My husband started walking towards it, and I said rather loudly, "Don't touch that petunia! It is God speaking to me."

I had been studying and meditating about planting seeds. One verse I had been meditating was Isaiah 61:11: "For as the earth brings forth its bud, as the garden causes the things that are sown in it to spring forth, so the Lord God will cause righteousness and praise to spring forth before all the nations."

The year before I had petunias planted in flower boxes at our windows. How did this little seed get in the crack in our patio and bloom? I don't know, but I know one thing. That petunia was there all summer and every time I looked at it, I saw life! I saw hope, and I felt the love of God shining on me as I remembered His faithfulness.

Just like that seed growing out of the crack in the brick patio, when we plant the Word of God in our heart, it has the power to split the hardest heart. It can grow and push the rubble and strongholds from our lives and bring the peace that passes all understanding.

God watches over His Word to make sure it is fulfilled. "For as the rain comes down, and the snow from heaven, and do not return there, but water the earth, and make it bring forth and bud, that it may give seed to the sower and bread to the eater, so shall My word be that goes forth from My mouth; it shall not return to Me void, but it shall accomplish what I please, and it shall prosper *in the thing* for which I sent it" (Isaiah 55:10-11).

The greatest gift God gave us besides Jesus is the Scriptures. In Psalm 138:2 we read, "For You have magnified Your word above all Your name."

"For the word of God *is* living and powerful, and sharper than any two-edged sword, piercing even to the division of soul and spirit, and of joints and marrow, and is a discerner of the thoughts and intents of the heart" (Hebrews 4:12). The Word is the seed. We plant it, we water it and we reap the harvest of understanding Kingdom principles, which the gates of hell cannot withstand.

The Word will always produce in good soil. It is always the condition of the soil that determines the harvest. The seed of God's Word has the power to penetrate a hardened heart and break the walls that we have built through insecurities and unbelief and change our lives.

The parable of the sower tells us, "A farmer went out to sow his seed. As he was scattering the seed, some fell along the path; it was trampled on, and the birds ate it up" (Luke 8:5 NIV). The soil in this heart was so hard that the seed could not penetrate the soil, leaving the seed on top of the soil where it became bird seed! Satan has total access to this soil.

How many times did you hear the gospel message and reject it? But one day someone's prayers caught up with you and you were ready to receive. Keep praying. Don't give up! My mother prayed for fifteen years for me, and one day it happened! I woke up crying. My husband, who had not received Christ asked, "What is wrong? We haven't gotten up, haven't said a word to each other and you are a mess!"

Well, I'm sure he did not expect what I asked: "Tell me how to be born again." He told me he had heard somewhere that you were to believe in your heart and confess with your mouth. I did and got up saved! He went back to sleep, a sinner. How can this happen? I was ready and he was the vehicle God chose to give me the message! I was his first convert, and he had no idea that he was called of God and would serve on the mission field! I'm sure that God was smiling over this thinking, "Just wait. Your life is going to change and never be the same again!"

The next soil Jesus talked about was rocky ground and thorns. "Those on the rocky ground are the ones who receive the word with joy when they hear it, but they have no root. They believe for a while, but in the time of testing they fall away. The seed that fell among thorns stands for those who hear, but as they go on their way they are choked by life's worries, riches and pleasures, and they do not mature" (Luke 8:13-14 NIV). The seed sown on rocky ground did not have the opportunity to grow a strong root system that would sustain it.

53

Pressures of the world had stopped the study and meditating of God's Word which waters the seed.

It takes time and commitment for a seed to grow and reap a harvest. We cannot allow the cares and anxieties of the world to distract us from our purpose in life to produce a harvest for the Kingdom of God.

When thorns are allowed to grow with the seed, they will choke the life from the seed, robbing it of the nutrients needed to complete the growth cycle. There are only enough nutrients to sustain either the seed or the weeds. The weeds have to be pulled from their root and destroyed. In other words, your focus will determine your growth.

The good news is that we have the ability to produce good soil.

"But the seed falling on good soil refers to someone *who hears the word and understands* it. This is the one who produces a crop, yielding a hundred, sixty or thirty times what was sown" (Matthew 13:23 NIV). Luke tells us this is a noble and good heart.

Understanding is the key. Understanding is power. Understanding comes when the Holy Spirit reveals a truth from the seed, the Word of God, to you. This is your harvest. The Holy Spirit reveals a truth from the Word producing faith in your life to please the Father. Hebrews 11:6 tells us, "But without faith it is impossible to please Him, for he who comes to God must believe that He is, and that He is a rewarder of those who diligently seek Him."

I believe your reward is revelation knowledge of the Word of God. Your faith grows as your heart perceives and understands spiritual realities from the Word of God. The unseen realm governs the visible realm and brings your mind into agreement with your heart and the reality of the Kingdom of God. This is renewing your mind to come into agreement with the reality of Heaven. When we are established in Kingdom principles, the anointing flows into the issues of life, directing our footsteps into the plans God has for our lives.

When Jesus told us we would have abundant life, He was not talking about an abundance of "things" in this world. He was speaking about joy and peace in the Holy Spirit. This is the atmosphere where you can hear His voice, and He clearly tells us in John 10:4, "He goes before them; and the sheep follow him, for they know his voice."

God knows we need "things" and that we humans "like things." And He is happy to lead us into a life where we have things, when things don't hold our heart. Matthew 6:33 is the key to obtaining your things in this world: "But seek first the kingdom of God and His righteousness, and all these things shall be added to you."

Faith is not believing for "things." It believes in a God who has promised to meet all of your needs. Most of us just don't understand what we need. We need joy and peace so we can hear His voice when He tells us to plant a seed that will meet our need. We will be obedient and reap a harvest. We are told in the Word to purpose in our heart what to give (2 Corinthians 9:7). We do this by asking Him to speak to our heart and guide us is our daily affairs.

Faith is the currency of Heaven and faith starts with a seed planted in your heart, watered with praise and thanksgiving, producing revelation of the hidden mysteries of the Kingdom of God. Matthew 13:11 says, "Because it has been given to you to know the mysteries of the kingdom of heaven, but to them it has not been given." As we stated before, truths are revealed to those who love the Lord God with all their heart and hunger and thirst for righteousness.

You, woman of God, are living at the corner of mystery and revelation! As you continue faithful in the Word, revelation attracts revelation in your life. We live in a corrupt world and the thief comes to steal, kill and destroy our joy and peace, distracting us with the cares of the world which will choke the seed planted in our hearts.

> *You, woman of God, are living at the corner of mystery and revelation!*

We are told to "fight the good fight of faith..." (1 Timothy 6:12). Sometimes we have to get down and get dirty to pull out the weeds of doubt and unbelief.

The woman with the issue of blood was a social outcast (Luke 8:43-48). For twelve years she went to physicians, spending all her livelihood to find help. She refused to give up! She heard Jesus was coming to her city, and she risked being in the crowd to touch the hem of His garment. She was desperate, and she was willing to look foolish in the eyes of man as she crawled on her knees to reach Jesus. She was willing to get down and get dirty to receive her miracle. Whatever had been stopping her healing was broken that day in the dirt of life!

When Jesus asked who had touched Him, she realized that she was not hidden and she came forth and confessed what she had done and why. His response, "Daughter, be of good cheer; your faith has made you well. Go in peace" (vs. 48). She had fought the good fight and won.

Faith is not a life of ease, but the rewards are out of this world! I believe the biggest enemies of our faith are discouragement and disappointment. We must learn to navigate the pain of life as we walk the runway of life.

As long as we live in this world, we are going to be in spiritual warfare. As we grow strong in the Lord, understand the mysteries of the Kingdom, learn about the weapons of our warfare and become skillful with our weapons, we can rest in the Lord because we understand the battle belongs to Him.

"For whatever is born of God overcomes the world. And this is the victory that has overcome the world – our faith" (1 John 5:4).

Your life reflects what you plant.

Points to Ponder:

- You alone are responsible for the soil of your heart.
- The Parable of the Sower holds a key to understand all other parables.
- Everything God does starts with a seed.
- Seedtime and harvest shall not cease.
- Understanding comes from revelation which gives you wisdom.

Faith plants the seed, Love makes them grow!

Chapter 5

Using the Fertilizer Dumped on Your Life

"Here on earth you will have many trials and sorrows. But take heart, because I have overcome the world."
John 16:33 NLT

Life is full of pain, but misery is optional to the woman of God. A Real Woman does not deny the trials and challenges of life, but she uses them to grow roses from the thorns of life.

A healthy rose bush not only produces more blooms, but is also better equipped to ward off disease and insects that try to kill its root system. Roses can learn to survive without fertilizer, but they struggle and usually just produce one bloom a season. They tend to adapt to their neglect and grow wild losing their sweet fragrance and deteriorate quickly.

Every situation that comes into our life is a warning signal that we need to adjust our lens in how we view life. Like the oil light in your car. If it comes on, you know you need to stop and check the oil level. The children of Israel became disheartened as they traveled around the same old mountain! "And the Lord spoke to me, saying: 'You have skirted this mountain long enough; turn northward' " (Deuteronomy 2:2-3). It is much easier to live in a rut than to break a habit or addiction. To break free of discouragement and disappointment. As you go around the mountain you know what to expect, you see the same people and hear the same old stories. You feed on each other in your pity parties.

But it is time to say enough is enough! You need to check the oil in your vessel. The oil of the Holy Spirit is hovering over you desiring to bring order from the chaos in your life. You have to step out of your comfort zone and take responsibility. We must use the trials and temptations that come into our life as fertilizer to cause us to turn to God and find His way of escape! "No temptation has overtaken you except such as is common to man; but God *is* faithful, who will not allow you to be tempted beyond what you are able, but with the temptation will also make the way of escape, that you may be able to bear *it*" (1 Corinthians 10:13).

The temptation for the child of God is to doubt God's Word. Does God really love me? If he loved me why am I going through this? When you feed on His Word, you know He will never leave you or forsake you and that nothing can separate you from the love of God. But when you are stuck in a rut, you need help. The Holy Spirit is your helper and all you have to do is cry out!

We all have dreams and expectations for life. We dream about that perfect man who will sweep us off our feet and all those perfect children, a successful career and ultimately live a long and happy life.

You have to give up the illusion that you deserve a life that is problem-free. This is false hope and living in a fantasy world.

When real life challenges start to batter your dreams and things are not as easy as you thought they would be, you can become weary in the battle. When storm clouds start rolling into your life, they can cloud your hope with disillusionment and change your focus and anticipation of your dreams. Your hope is deferred by these clouds of doubt, creating an unhealthy climate around you with a stormy forecast for your future.

Proverbs 13:12 says, "Hope deferred makes the heart sick, but *when* the desire comes, *it is* a tree of life."

When our dreams are battered with real life challenges, you are betrayed by a friend, someone lies about you, or you lose your job which has many negative effects on your life, clouds of despair take the sunshine from your dreams and hope is deferred. We start to question our desires and wonder why God is taking so long. Does He really love me? These thoughts bring us to a place of temptation. Do we really trust God?

A deferred dream is not a failure; it is an opportunity for a divine encounter with God. This is a place where we learn to wait upon the Lord. Isaiah 40:31 tells us, "But those who wait upon the Lord shall renew their strength; they shall mount up with wings as eagles; they shall run and not be weary, and they shall walk and not faint."

Waiting is one of the most difficult things to do for those who have put their total trust in God. We want what we want now! But, waiting on God is one thing I have learned that He requires of us who have put our hope and trust in Him.

This season of our life is where character is formed, giving us the strength to endure in our time of temptation. When we choose to wait we are saying, "Lord, I trust You." Waiting is the process of allowing God to work in us for His good pleasure. (See Philippians 2:13). What He does in us as we wait is more important than what we are waiting on!

Romans 5:3-5 NLT gives us the pattern to build hope in our life: "We can rejoice, too, when we run into problems and trials, for we know that they help us develop endurance. And endurance develops strength of character, and character strengthens our confident hope of salvation. And this hope will not lead to disappointment. For we know how dearly God loves us, because he has given us the Holy Spirit to fill our hearts with his love."

Hope starts with dreams, visions and expectations; and when they meet with the storm clouds of life, we find ourselves in a place where we don't understand what is going on. This is a place where many people give up, and their heart becomes sick with bitterness. Anger takes root, and you are mad at God. You have lost hope.

This is a time when you have to make a choice to trust God and declare His faithfulness. It is a time for Proverbs 20:24 (TLB) to become revelation in your heart: "Since the Lord is directing our steps, why try to understand everything that happens along the way?" This is the first scripture that God opened my eyes to as a young Christian. I'm sure He knew how often I would need this Word. "Lord, since You are directing my steps, I will not try to understand what is happening along the way!" I could not tell you how many times in the last forty years I have said that!

As you are walking in this season trusting God, you will

develop endurance. Godly character is being formed in you, bringing you to a place of hope! And hope will not disappoint!

When the Lord delivered the children of Israel out of Egypt and told them about the Promised Land, He told them He would not give them the land all at once. There were many giants in the land that they did not know how to fight. He knew they would be consumed by the enemy. He was protecting them. He was telling them as they increased He would drive out the enemies. (See Exodus 23:29-30)

They did not know how to fight to possess the promises of God. They had a slave mentally, and they had to increase in the knowledge of the Lord to be prepared for the battle. The same is true for us. When we are born again and walking in the new creation life, we must understand the mysteries of the Kingdom of Heaven and how to access God's world so we can change the world in which we live (See Matthew 13:11).

At the same time, He kept them in the wilderness. He directed their footsteps with a cloud and with fire. He fed them with manna. God will never leave you or forsake you, no matter what your thoughts and emotions are saying to you. " And they overcame him by the blood of the Lamb and by the word of their testimony, and they did not love their lives to the death" (Revelation 12:11). That is why we declare and decree what God has spoken. When we do this, it is an invitation for a divine encounter with the Holy Spirit to bring sunshine back into our life and restore our hope!

We must protect the environment of our heart. by continually planting the seeds of His Word in our heart. Psalm 119:105 tells us, "Your word *is* a lamp to my feet and a light to my path."

You don't have to stumble in this world; turn on the light. He will tell you when to take the next step and lead you through the detours of life.

Leah understood about the trials of life. She was a substitute bride, betrayed by her father, rejected by her husband and hated by her sister. Can it get much worse? They all lived together. She faced them every day!

She understood about the pain of life, but she was a woman who fulfilled her destiny in life. Ruth 4:11 tells us, "...Rachel and Leah, the two who built the house of Israel. . . ."

Leah grew up obscured by the shadow of a beautiful sister. She was very aware that all heads turned toward Rachel. When the dashing Jacob came into their home, he had eyes only for Rachel, the beautiful younger sister. Jacob agreed to work seven years just to marry Rachel. Leah, the older sister, was not considered by Jacob. When it came time for the wedding, Laban, Leah's father, knew that it was very unlikely that any young man would ask for Leah's hand, so he decided that she would be a substitute bride. Can you imagine her wedding night? There were many questions going through her mind: How will Jacob respond when he finds out the truth? Will he keep her or refuse to stay with her? How was Rachel responding? She had also been deceived.

Leah had learned to cope with pain early in life. She understood she had to face the reality of her situation. Even though her marriage to Jacob came by trickery, Leah was legally Jacob's wife—and his first wife at that. Leah had become a victim.

Today many women find themselves in the victim situation. There is only one answer—forgiveness. Forgiveness is not about the abuser; it is about setting you free from the power of the abuser. Only the Holy Spirit can help you forgive, and you must ask for His help. You are not alone; the Holy Spirit is with you. First John 1:9 tells us, "If we confess our sins, He is faithful and just to forgive us *our* sins and to cleanse us from all unrighteousness."

Forgiveness is instant, but the cleansing takes time. That is why when a thought enters your mind about the situation and you feel pain or regret, the devil will try to tell you that you didn't forgive or you wouldn't feel this way. It takes time to cleanse your heart from the hurt. As you continue reading the Word, asking the Holy Spirit to take away the pain, you will be cleansed by the washing of the Word of God (Ephesians 5:26).

Forgiveness is instant, but the cleansing takes time.

We can see the Lord working in Leah and on her behalf as she names her children. Here Leah expresses her true feelings. Each name reflects the honest yearning of her heart and the hope that is within her.

In naming her first son Reuben, meaning "the Lord has looked on my affliction," she knew that God had seen her situation and what she was going through. The faithfulness of God is expressed in the naming of her second son, Simeon—"one who hears." She knew that God had heard her heart cry and was with her and would never leave her. Every time she called Reuben and Simeon, she was reminded that the Lord knew where she was, what she was going through and that He was with her.

In naming her third son, we see that Leah still longed to be loved by Jacob. His name, Levi, means "attached." Her heart burst with her desire when she said, "Now this time my husband will become attached to me, because I have borne him three sons" (Genesis 29:34). Can you hear her pain, the longing in her heart for the love of her husband?

Imagine her pain. Obviously, Jacob had continued to be a husband to her, because she conceived three times and bore him children. And yet, there was still obvious distance between them.

Rachel, her sister, seemed to have everything going her way. But underneath her beauty was a heart of envy. She saw the blessing of God on Leah and was jealous. She turned bitter towards Leah. Not only did Leah have to cope with the pain of rejection from her husband, but also the hatred of her sister and the betrayal of her father. What a family!

Yet, this family is the one God used to build the house of Israel. Despite the chaos and dysfunction of this family, the twelve tribes of Israel came and God's purpose is still being fulfilled.

The testimony of this family should encourage you and give you hope. God uses ordinary people and works through their problems to establish His purpose on the earth. We do not have to be perfect, but we do need to be persistent!

The time of testing and sorrow enriched Leah's life. The absence of her husband's love and the hatred of her sister brought her to a greater understanding of God's love and acceptance.

The birth of her fourth son, Judah, shows us that Leah had walked through her pain and sorrow to victory. God turned a negative situation into something good. "Now I will praise the

Lord," she exclaims! (Genesis 29:35). She named this son Judah meaning "praise." For the first time she was not showing signs of her hurt and expectation of Jacob to meet her needs. She had put her total trust in God, and understood that no man on earth could fulfill all of her needs.

Leah did not understand the prophetic meaning of the moment. Judah was the start of a new beginning both for her and for the world. From the descendants of the tribe of Judah, Jesus the Messiah would come. Leah didn't realize how privileged she was. Though rejected by man, she was chosen by God!

What happened to Leah? She had a heart change! She had cultivated the soil of her heart, tearing up the roots of bitterness, rejection and betrayal. As she walked through the pain, she knew that God saw her affliction and He had heard her cry. Little by little, as she kept her heart turned towards God, a change was taking place within her heart. Her confidence and faith in God's love grew until it poured forth out of her heart. She saw the faithfulness of God in the birth of her children.

Rachel also lived a life of pain and sorrow. Her frustration is evident when she became the first to offer her maid to Jacob to at least have children for her. Unlike Leah, Rachel did not come to a place in her life where she submitted to the will of God and to trust Him to work out His plan for her life.

Despite the opening of her womb with Joseph's birth, it was years before she conceived again. This time, her longed-for son took her life just as he was entering the world. With her dying breath she named him Ben-oni, which means "the son of my sorrow." Jacob called him Benjamin, and mourned passionately for Rachel. She did not live to nurture and care for the sons she fought to produce. She had Jacob's undying love and adoration, but never fully rested in it.

Things are not always what they look like on the outside. Don't envy a person who seems to have it all together. No one has an easy life. Only through the grace of God can we cope in this world—regardless of circumstances.

I believe Jacob came to appreciate the beauty of Leah and had many cherished memories of their life together. When Jacob called his sons together to bless them, he told them that Leah had been buried in the family burial cave at Machpelah. At her death Leah was given a place of honor alongside Abraham, Sarah, Isaac and Rebekah. Her rejection was over—though she had no doubt put it to rest many years before because of the choices she made in dealing with her life's challenges.

Jacob had been attracted to Rachel because of her outward beauty, but God had been attracted to Leah for her inner beauty. In the midst of Leah's problems, while she is still working through the pain of life, God is leading her through her purpose in life for His Kingdom.

Leah's heart had been transformed by the power of God. The preparation of the heart belongs to man, but the Lord's purpose will prevail. We must learn to cultivate the soil of our heart to receive the seed of God's Word which brings healing and hope for the future to grow roses from the thorns of life.

"The entrance of Your words gives light;
It gives understanding to the simple".
Psalms 119:130

Points to Ponder:

- Trials and temptation are common to life.
- We use the trials and temptation for fertilizer for growth in our spiritual walk.
- A delayed dream is not a failure; it is an opportunity for a divine encounter with God.
- Hope does not disappoint.
- Character is formed as we wait upon the Lord

Chapter 6

Cultivating the Soil of Your Heart

"Plow up the hard ground of your hearts!
Do not waste your good seed among thorns."
Jeremiah 4:3 NLT

As I studied about rose bushes, I learned that they had to be tended to regularly. If not fed and watered consistently, the bush will become overgrown, producing inferior blooms. A rose bush that is under stress from any source—lack of food and water or insect attack—will stop blooming. Roses love sunlight. The more sunshine they get, the healthier the plant producing more roses.

We must continually expose the soil of our heart to the influences of God's Word and the fresh breath of the Holy Spirit. The soil of our heart must be nourished with spiritual light and warmth with the soft showers of His grace.

Seeds that are planted in hard ground will only produce thorns in your life that hinder growth and produce pain. Watering your garden with the Word of God aerates the soil that is hard packed and snips the dead buds to make room for new buds.

You must uproot, tear down and destroy weeds of the past. Roots of resentment, bitterness and unforgiveness will choke the life out of you. Seeds of selfishness, greed and envy will harden your heart and bring death to dreams and hopes for your future. If we neglect the garden of our heart, it soon becomes overgrown with thoughts of doom and gloom and no longer reflects the beauty of God's glory.

*You **must** uproot, tear down and destroy weeds of the past.*

How do you start your day? Do you look forward to another day in the Kingdom of God, trusting Him to work out all the details to keep peace in your life? Or do you dread getting out of bed, allowing your thoughts to run wild, forecasting gloom and doom for your day.

Maintaining a consistent lifestyle of watering the garden of your heart the first thing in the morning when everything is fresh prepares you for another active day.

As you pray and kill the weeds of doubt and unbelief, you make a way for sunlight to warm the soil of your heart and even highlight areas that need better tending in your life.

Fresh manna every morning gives life and strength to your soul and spirit, giving you a clear mind and a sensitive heart to lead your body through the detours of life.

The Word of God is life and light; without it we will stumble in this world. Jesus understood this when He said in John 16:1, "These things I have spoken to you, that you should not be made to stumble." He continues in John 15:11 and John 16:33 telling us the value of His Word and why He spoke to us—that our joy would be full and that we could overcome the world.

Are you getting the message? Without the Word of God hidden in our heart, without putting the Word of God first and making it a priority, we will stumble in the world, living a frustrated and defeated life because the soil of our heart is hard.

We are always learning and growing as long as we tend to the garden of our heart and plant the seed of His Word into good ground. This is the most important thing we can do. Remember one of our key scriptures: "Above all else, guard your heart, for everything you do flows from it" (Proverbs 4:23 NIV).

In every garden, there is only one source of life: God. When we make the decision to have a daily devotional life, the fruit of our time at His feet will be a peaceful life.

Remember, Jesus said, "But one thing is needed, and Mary has chosen that good part, which will not be taken away from her" (Luke 10:42). Most people don't understand what they really need. The Word of God is life, and life flows from the heart! Mary received insight because she chose the good part, and it was not taken away from her. Like Mary, we must make a habit of sitting at Jesus' feet.

Yes, there will be challenges and struggles in life, but just like Jesus, you will walk through them and go on about your day.

A well-tended heart will bud and bloom continually through every season of your life.

We need to keep our garden tools sharp to cultivate and root out the thorns of life that are trying to destroy our purpose and destiny.

Praise and worship is a powerful tool that will cause your enemy to run! When praise fills your mouth and you enter God's gates with thanksgiving, the enemy will run! This is how you torment your enemy and clear your mind of distracting thoughts.

Psalm 100:4 says, "Enter into His gates with thanksgiving, *and* into His courts with praise. Be thankful to Him, *and* bless His name." Thanksgiving gets the ear of heaven and turns our heart towards God. Thanksgiving is the force that moves the mountain!

"Therefore by Him let us continually offer the sacrifice of praise to God, that is, the fruit of *our* lips, giving thanks to His name" (Hebrews 13:15). You have been clothed with a garment of praise for the spirit of heaviness (Isaiah 61:3). When you wear your garment of praise, you are clothed in victory, and deliverance becomes a reality!

The sacrifice of praise acknowledges that God's faithfulness and goodness are more real to you than the trial you are facing in this world. This is an expression of your faith and has the power to transform you.

First Thessalonians 5:16-18 is also a very important scripture for our daily living and how to guard our heart in this world: "Rejoice always, pray without ceasing, in everything give thanks, for this is the will of God in Christ Jesus for you." Notice, it says "in everything," not "for everything."

Rejoicing, praying and giving thanks are all about "heart"

attitudes. It is an act of our will, an attitude of humility.

There is no reason for the fruit of your labor to ever wilt or die, as it is the everlasting reflection of God's goodness and His abundance. A well-tended heart has beautiful thoughts that continually produce a harvest!

We are warned in the Word about having a hardened heart. Hebrews 3:8 tells us, "Do not harden your hearts as in the rebellion." Verse 10 says, "They always go astray in their heart, and they have not known My ways." Verse 12 tells us, "Beware, brethren, lest there be in any of you an evil heart of unbelief in departing from the living God." We need to heed these words.

A hard heart will not see or hear the voice of the Lord.

I love the testimonies of feeding the five thousand and then the four thousand. Jesus used the disciples in these two miracles. The food passed through their hands to the people, and they still did not understand what happened!

Mark 6:52 says, "For they had not understood about the loaves, because their heart was hardened." They walked and talked with Jesus every day, but their hearts were hardened!

In Mark, chapter 8, after feeding the four thousand, when they were departing in a boat, the disciples had forgotten to take bread with them, except for one loaf. Jesus spoke to them in verses 17-21 and said:

"Why do you reason because you have no bread? Do you not yet perceive nor understand? Is your heart still hardened? Having eyes, do you not see? And having ears, do you not hear? And do you not remember? When I broke the five loaves for the five thousand, how many baskets full of fragments did you take up?" They said to Him, "Twelve." "Also, when I broke the seven for the four thousand, how many large baskets full of fragments did you take up?" "And they said, "Seven." So He said to them, "How is it you do not understand?"

If your heart is hard, you can be in the middle of a great outpouring of the Holy Spirit and not have any idea what is happening!

Do you not see?

Do you not hear?

Do you not remember?

You need to ask yourself these three questions. These symptoms are all signs of a hardened heart.

Do you not remember? God understood how easily we forget things. That is why He was always telling the children of Israel to build a memorial. Take twelve stones from the Jordan River, Why? So when they passed by they would remember, and they could tell generations to come about the miracles of the Lord.

Jesus also understood the importance of remembering. In Luke 22:19 after breaking bread for the disciples He said, "This is My body which is given for you; do this in remembrance of Me." When you are receiving communion, what do you remember? Communion has a purpose. It is a time when we stop and think on the goodness of God and thank Him for what He has done and is doing in our life.

Remembering is another garden tool used to cultivate the soil of our hearts. When I was reading Philippians 3:13 one day where Paul says, "But one thing I do, forgetting those things which are behind and reaching forward for those things which are ahead," I was pondering in my heart, thinking, "If this was the 'one' thing Paul did, I should also forget the things which are behind." My thought was, "How do I forget?" The devil is constantly reminding me of everything wrong I have done!

The Lord immediately spoke to me and said, "You remember." This seemed odd to me. Forget and remember. Aren't they opposites? Then the Lord spoke again, "When you remember, you choose your thoughts." If you are not choosing your thoughts, then the enemy is filling your head.

Your remembrance in the new creation life starts at the cross.

We can learn from the children of Israel. Psalm 78:40-43 tells us: "How often they provoked Him in the wilderness, and grieved Him in the desert! Yes, again and again they tempted God, and limited the Holy One of Israel. They did not remember His power: The day when He redeemed them from the enemy, when He worked His signs in Egypt, and His wonders in the field of Zoan."

They limited the Holy One of Israel because they did not remember. This is amazing to me! I have a forty-year history with God. My history with God is what gives me the endurance to wait upon the Lord! When I am tempted to doubt God, I remember when He brought deliverance and turned a bad situation into good.

I can imagine as they walked through the Red Sea, rejoicing at their deliverance, and saying, "I will never forget this!" But when their stomachs started to grumble, they soon forgot!

Thanksgiving and remembrance go together and have the power to pull weeds that are deep within our heart.

Life is a journey; it is not a problem to solve. If we keep an open heart and walk in obedience, we will be flowing in the beauty of His presence every day.

What we must understand is that our enemy has only one weapon—deception. As long as we are in this world, it will be a continuous battle of good versus evil. As we grow in the Word and understand our spiritual armor (Ephesians, chapter 6), we will discern the tactics of the devil and can stop his assaults with the weapons of our warfare.

Jesus came to destroy the works of the devil. First John 3:8 tells us, "For this purpose the Son of God was manifested, that He might destroy the works of the devil."

We also know that satan is the god of this world (2 Corinthians 4:4). As children of God, we have been given authority as Jesus shared in Luke 10:19: " Behold, I give you the authority to trample on serpents and scorpions, and over all the power of the enemy, and nothing shall by any means hurt you."

> *It is our responsibility to use our authority to stop satan's work in our lives.*

Prayer is one of the most powerful forces in the world to cultivate the weeds of doubt and unbelief in our garden. Prayer is talking with God and having a conversation with Him. It is inquiring of the Lord in our time of need. It should be easy to talk with our Best Friend.

*What a Friend we have in Jesus, all our sins and griefs
to bear! What a privilege to carry everything
to God in prayer! O what peace we often forfeit,
O what needless pain we bear,
All because we do not carry everything to God in prayer.*

I love this hymn. I can always feel the heart of the one who penned it. This is a hymn from the heart that gives life to the hearers, even after generations.

Prayer is our communication with God. When we pray, it shows that we have confidence in God.

"Now this is the confidence that we have in Him, that if we ask anything according to His will, He hears us. And if we know that He hears us, whatever we ask, we know that we have the petitions that we have asked of Him" (1 John 5:14-15).

Yes, we can know that we have the petitions that we ask of Him. When His peace fills our heart, we know that we know that all is well and we have the answers to our petitions.

The secret of asking is abiding. "If you abide in Me, and My words abide in you, *you will ask* what you desire, and it shall be done for you" (John 15:7). *IF you abide!* When your heart is abiding in His Word, asking is an automatic response to whatever problem you face in your journey of life.

Philippians 4:6-8 says: " Be anxious for nothing, but in everything by prayer and supplication, with thanksgiving, let your requests be made known to God; and the peace of God, which surpasses all understanding, will guard your hearts and minds through Christ Jesus."

The key in this scripture is "with thanksgiving." Again, we are talking about a heart attitude, remembering, thanksgiving and prayer go hand in hand. When I remember what God has done in my life, it fills my heart with thanksgiving and gives me the faith to endure while I'm waiting on the next prayer to be answered.

Rebekah was a strong woman of faith and prayer. She was willing to leave all, her family and country, when Abraham's servant came looking for a wife for Isaac. This is a beautiful love story that began the moment they saw each other in the field.

Rebekah became pregnant and felt a struggle within her. "She said, 'If *all is* well, why *am I like* this?'" *So she went to inquire of the Lord.* And the Lord said to her: "Two nations *are* in your womb, two peoples shall be separated from your body; *one* people shall be stronger than the other, and the older shall serve the younger" (Genesis 25:22-23). Rebekah knew that according to the custom of her culture, it was impossible for the older to serve the younger.

I can relate to Rebekah when she said, "If all is well, why am I like this?" I'm sure you can too. She inquired of the Lord and received a prophetic word for the future.

The boys grew and one day she overheard Isaac talking with Esau about the blessing that was needed with the birthright for him to become a leader. She immediately started making plans for Jacob to deceive Isaac so he would receive the blessing. (See Genesis, chapter 27).

What happened to this woman of faith who had inquired of the Lord in her time of need? Somehow over the years she had become weary. Maybe she had not been accepted by the people in this land and was lonely. Whatever had happened, her heart had been clouded, and she did not inquire of the Lord seeking help in her time of need.

I believe the answer is in Genesis 25:28: "And Isaac loved Esau because he ate *of his* game, but Rebekah loved Jacob." There was division in the home, and division is the doorway for deception. Favoritism was a curse that followed the family line for generations.

We see it in Jacob's family. Joseph was favored by his father and was given a beautiful coat. He loved that coat and wore it all the time, no matter what the temperature was! His brothers hated him and the coat! It was a constant reminder to them that he was the favored son and got by with everything and evidently did what he wanted. Why wasn't he with his brothers tending the flocks?

Then he had a dream, and instead of meditating and seeking the Lord for direction, he tells his family about it, adding insult to the already tense family situation. Psalm 105:19 tells us, "Until the time that his word came to pass, the word of the Lord tested him." It was thirteen years from the dream to the fulfilment of it. We know during this time he was thrown in a pit by his brothers, and he later had a prison ministry before he entered the palace.

During his time in the pit, Joseph began to think about his life and his family. Joseph was not perfect and needed some personal ministry. Perhaps a little pride had entered in as he strutted around wearing his coat. He was hurt by his brothers. He didn't understand what was going on. The coat gave him a sense of importance, something he could use against his brothers.

The longer Joseph sat in that pit, he began to see some faults in his life. When he repented, God sent a camel train going to Egypt to pick him up and further his time of training for the call of leadership on his life.

Read and study this family. You will relate to many situations in their lives. They were far from perfect people, yet God was able to work through all their problems for His purpose.

The world is hard, but we must protect the garden of our heart with fellowship with like believers, prayer for one another, not allowing ourselves to be separated. It is the banana that gets separated from the bunch that gets peeled!

Sharpen your garden tools, cultivate your heart and prepare for the harvest!

When flowers bloom, faith grows!

Points to Ponder:

- You must uproot, tear down and destroy weeds of the past.
- How do you start your day? Maintain a consistent lifestyle of watering the garden of your heart the first thing each morning to prepare yourself for another day.
- Fresh manna every morning gives life and strength to your spirit and soul, giving you a clear mind, making you alert to detours in your life.
- Praise, thanksgiving and remembering are garden tools to cultivate the soil of your heart.
- Prayer gives God the place to guide you through the trials of life.

Chapter 7

Building a Strong Root System

"But David strengthened himself in the Lord his God."
1 Samuel 30:6

The beauty of the rose is determined by its root structure. As we feast on the beauty of the rose it is easy to forget that its beauty started underground. The quality of the rose is also determined by the health of the root structure.

The root system is very fragile until it grows strong enough to bring stability to the life of the rose bush. As the root system is fed and brings strength to the plant it will be able to fight the pests and disease that endanger the plant. A layer of mulch will protect the roots and stop weeds from stealing nutrients from the plant. A good root structure will keep the plant stable in all the seasons of life. A long hard winter can damage the plant and cause it to produce an inferior blossom if the root structure is not protected.

Diligence and consistent care of the root system brings forth a healthy plant to share its beauty with the world. A plant that is unattended will grow wild and cannot support itself from the thorns of life.

The tools that we studied in the previous chapter are like mulch to our spirit and soul that are needed to protect our heart. Praise and worship, thanksgiving and remembering the faithfulness of God guards our heart and gives us the courage to face the trials of life. As we steward our heart we must build a strong foundation that will not allow the winds of adversity to steal the desires of our heart.

As we look at David's life, we see that he walked through many years of testing. His character was being formed to face the giants of life. His private victories, as he was tending his father's sheep, gave him the strength to face the giant. He had been rooted and grounded and established in his faith as he was alone in the fields, overcoming the rejection of his family and friends. When Samuel came looking to anoint one of Jesse' sons as king, David had not even been considered.

I personally believe that is what set David apart from others was his ability to strengthen himself in the Lord. When no one else was around and there were no prayer meetings to attend, he was standing all alone. In the midst of betrayal he was able to look past the offense and strengthen himself in the Lord. We have much to learn from the life of David, a man after God's heart (Acts 13:22).

We must grasp the fact that as a child of God we live in the natural and the supernatural. We have to learn how to live from heaven to earth. Awareness of the unseen things is a vital part of our new creation life. Colossians 3:2-3 tells us, "Set your mind on things above, not on things on the earth. For you died, and your life is hidden with Christ in God." The abundant life that Jesus promised is found in the unseen realm. We must learn to access His world to change our world. Only those that can see the invisible can do the impossible!

> *The abundant life that Jesus promised*
> *is found in the unseen realm.*

Jesus said, "...the kingdom of God is within you" (Luke 17:21). All kingdom issues are heart issues. That is why we must guard our heart, above all else! We must learn to deal with attitudes, ambitions and agendas in this world. Our relationship with the Holy Spirit is foundational in obtaining the breakthrough that we are looking for in this world.

Joshua 1:8 gives us a clue to having a successful life in the natural realm. "Study this Book of Instruction continually. meditate on it day and night so you will be sure to obey everything written in it. Only then will you prosper and succeed in all you do" (NLT).

Meditation brings revelation. As we meditate the Word of God our mind is being renewed as the Holy Spirit brings revelation from the scriptures that impart life as they become a living Word to us.

When the Holy Spirit releases knowledge it enables us to address specific issues in our life at crucial moments. Jesus told us in Matthew 13:11 that it had been given to us to know the mysteries of the Kingdom of Heaven.

Revelation means "to lift the veil." Revelation knowledge leads us to an encounter with God that brings personal transformation in our lives. Revelation knowledge is what sets our mind on things above!

The Holy Spirit unveils what has been freely given to us by God to enable us to navigate the runway of life.

1 Corinthians 2:10-12 tells us, "But God has revealed *them* to us through His Spirit. For the Spirit searches all things, yes, the deep things of God. For what man knows the things of a man except the spirit of the man which is in him? Even so no one knows the things of God except the Spirit of God. Now we have received, not the spirit of the world, but the Spirit who is from God, *that we might know the things that have been freely given to us by God.*"

Paul understood the value of revelation as he shares in Ephesians 3:3-5 NIV, "that is, the mystery made known to me by revelation, as I have already written briefly. In reading this, then, you will be able to understand my insight into the mystery of Christ, which was not made known to people in other generations as it has now been revealed by the Spirit to God's holy apostles and prophets."

The Word of God that has been revealed to our spirit (heart) can never be taken away from us. It is when we know that we know there is absolutely nothing that can separate us from the love of God. The revealed Word in our heart is the foundation of our faith! You must pursue the truth of God's Word with passion. Truth comes from revelation knowledge and the truth will set you free! (John 8:32)

We must continue praying as Paul prayed in Ephesians 1:17,

"That the God of our Lord Jesus Christ, the Father of glory may give to you the spirit of wisdom and revelation in the knowledge of Him." We thrive on revelation knowledge and dry up without it!

We thrive on revelation knowledge and dry up without it!

Our purpose in life is to know Him and the power of His resurrection. "so that I may know Him [experientially, becoming more thoroughly acquainted with Him, understanding the remarkable wonders of His Person more completely] and [in that same way experience] the power of His resurrection [which overflows and is active in believers], and [that I may share] the fellowship of His sufferings, by being continually conformed [inwardly into His likeness even] to His death [dying as He did]" (Philippians 3:10 AMP).

Our righteousness, right standing with God, is provided for us in Jesus Christ, and it is a complete and perfect righteousness that we obtain by faith in Christ's blood that we are made conformable to Christ's death, when we die to sin, as he died for sin; and the world is crucified to us, and we to the world, by the cross of Christ.

Accepting Jesus puts us in right standing with God. Receiving the Holy Spirit gives us the power to live in right standing with God.

Paul was willing to suffer hardship, rejection and betrayal in this world to gain souls for the Kingdom of God. He understood spiritual warfare and that he was not fighting flesh and blood but spiritual rulers of darkness in heavenly places.

We must build a strong root system in the knowledge of the truth of His Word that will lead us into the plans and purpose for our life. Building a strong root system takes time. It is a daily walk with Jesus. God delights in showing His love to us along the way to encourage us through the trials of life.

Recently returning from a busy trip, I was extremely tired. As I was walking to the gate for our flight, I said to my husband, "I would really like to upgrade to first class." When we were at our gate waiting for the airplane, suddenly I heard, "will Joyce and Bill Tilney come to the desk for a message." As I was walking up to the desk a young man met me and handed me new boarding passes and said, "I upgraded you to first class." As I stood there with my mouth hanging open, I said, "thank you Jesus." I returned to our seats and told my husband, "we have just been kissed by God!"

Proverbs 29:18 tells us, "Where *there is* no revelation, the people cast off restraint; but happy *is* he who keeps the law." The impact of revelation knowledge in a person's life is what keeps them from falling into the temptation of every wind of doctrine that comes against the purpose of their life.

As a child of God we walk in the revelation we have received in the midst of mysteries that we cannot explain. That is why Christianity is called the walk of faith. The Holy Spirit knows exactly when to breathe on the Word you need and as you increase more will be given. Revelation attracts revelation.

As we focus on strengthening ourselves in the Lord and building a strong root system, Jude 1:20 instructs us in building ourselves up in our faith. "But you, beloved, building yourselves up on your most holy faith, praying in the Holy Spirit." Another scripture, 1 Corinthians 14:4 tells us, "He who speaks in a tongue edifies himself..." The word edifies means to build up.

When we use our tongue to give voice to utterance from our spirit, which is in communion with the Holy Spirit, we are praying the perfect will of God.

1 Corinthians 14:2 tells us, "For he who speaks in a tongue does not speak to men but to God, for no one understands *him;* however, in the spirit he speaks mysteries." When we pray in tongues we are praying from the new nature given to us when we were born again which is in total agreement with God

As we engage our mind and body in praying in the spirit, we begin to experience a greater reality in the natural of what our spirit already knows. When we received Jesus, the Holy Spirit in us knows all things. We have to pull from what is given to us when we are born again, to walk in the Spirit in this world. God has already given us everything we need pertaining to life and Godliness.(2 Peter 1: 2-4) We have to learn to live from the inside out.

Praying in the spirit is a powerful tool that keeps our focus from being distracted from the things of the world. As we lean into the presence of the Holy Spirit, we can hear that whisper of the Lord which strengthens us in our time of need.

Daniel 10:19 says, "So when he spoke to me I was strengthened, and said, "Let my lord speak, for you have strengthened me." We must hear His voice to follow Him. John 10:27 says,

"My sheep hear My voice, and I know them, and they follow Me." To hear His voice, you have to learn to listen and not be distracted by the many other voices in this world. I am desperate to hear His voice! Every morning before my feet hit the ground; I start my day with thanksgiving and ask the Lord to give me a "fresh word" to feed my spirit that day.

Like Paul, I am thankful that I can pray with the spirit and be strengthened in my time of need. "Therefore, my brothers and sisters, be eager to prophesy, and do not forbid speaking in tongues" (1 Corinthians 14:39 NIV)

Ephesians 6:10-18 is all about spiritual warfare. Verse 18 tells us, "*And pray in the Spirit* on all occasions with all kinds of prayers and requests. With this in mind, be alert and always keep on praying for all the Lord's people" (NIV).

As I pray in the spirit, peace comes and I can think clearly and hear the voice of God to lead me through any situation I find myself in. Praying in the spirit is part of my daily walk with the Lord. This is spiritual warfare

"What is *the conclusion* then? I will pray with the spirit, and I will also pray with the understanding. I will sing with the spirit, and I will also sing with the understanding" (1 Corinthians 14:15).

Fear is real. We are told in 2 Timothy 2:7, "For God has not given us a spirit of fear, but of power and of love and of a sound mind." Notice it is a "spirit" of fear. Second Corinthians 4:13 speaks to us about a "spirit of faith." We have a choice, we are either going to walk in faith or fear. Whichever we agree with, fear or faith, we will obey (Romans 6:16).

Satan is always trying to deceive us into agreeing with him

which empowers him in our life. When you believe a lie, you empower the liar. This is what happened in the Garden and continues to this day. Satan must entice us into agreement with him to gain access into our life to kill, steal and destroy. As we walk in this dark world, fear is real, and we must learn how to fight it.

When we are suddenly faced with trauma or bad news in our life, fear will try to overcome us. We will be faced with the temptation to doubt God's Word. When you feel fear, you must pause, take a deep breath and start praying in the spirit. This is the best way I have learned to overcome fear.

Christian life can feel overwhelming at times. We are to attend church regularly, pray without ceasing, evangelize our neighborhoods and workplace, along with taking mission trips! And then there is the discipline of the Christian life; personal Bible study, praying, meditating the Word as we build a career and care for a family as we continue in spiritual warfare! During all of this you keep a smile on your face and enjoy your life!

A great man of wisdom, Solomon gave us a wonderful word of wisdom for our life. "*Above all else*, guard your heart, for everything you do flows from it" (Proverbs 4:23 NIV). The theme of this book flows around this scripture. Above all else means above all else! You don't have to give in to the pressure of man, when your heart is right, God will lead you and you will fulfill your purpose in life.

Early in my Christian walk I had done something I realized was wrong. I was upset with myself, God spoke to me, "*I will bless your ignorance when your heart is right.*" He then lead me to Proverbs 4:23. From that point I have diligently sought the

Lord for His help in teaching me to guard my heart.

We must set priorities in our life. God is first, your family second and your work and ministry third. As you put God first you will be guarding your heart and be in a position where God can guide you in your life. God knows where you are, what you are going through and when you are ready for promotion.

"Therefore do not cast away your confidence, which has great reward. For you have need of endurance, so that after you have done the will of God, you may receive the promise" (Hebrews 10:35-36).

It just takes one day for everything to turn around. It might be 20 years in the making, but it happens in one day!

The testimony of the Shunammite woman is one of great endurance as she walked through the pain of life to receive the desire of her heart (2 Kings 4:8-37; 2 Kings 8:1-6).

She was a notable woman married to an older man. She had longed for children, but was barren. In her culture this brought great shame to her life. Month after month she waited for her womb to be opened and bless her husband with a son. She suffered rejection and gossip from the neighbors. She felt insignificant and like a failure.

It happened one day that she noticed a man of God walking past her home. She told her husband about this man and asked him to build a small upper room on the roof for him to rest. (vs.8-10)

It happened one day that he turned into her home to rest. As he rested he had the desire to do something for her. He told his servant, Gehazi to call her and ask what they could do for her. "Do you want me to speak on your behalf to the king or to the commander of the army?" She answered, *"I dwell among my own people"* (vs.11-13).

Elisha asked his servant, "What can we do?" His servant brought to his attention the fact that she had no son and her husband was old. He called to her again and told her "about this time next year you shall embrace a son. "No my lord, Man of God, do not lie to your maidservant." The woman did conceive and gave birth to a son. (vs.16)

I'm always amazed as I read her response. "I dwell among my own people" She had learned to be content with her life. She had accepted her situation and overcome the hurt and heartache of being barren. Her answer, "do not lie to your maidservant," is very strong words. She had accepted her position; she was happy with her life and was being used by God to minister to His servant, Elisha. She did not want to go down that path again.

It is okay to tell God how you feel. He knows anyway and He desires that you be open and honest with Him. You are not going to make God mad! Read the Psalms, David continually shared his struggle in life, but he always picked himself up and ended praising the Lord. God understands that we are human and that we have to grow in the knowledge of God to overcome in this world.

Her son grew and went with his father to the fields. *One day* he complained of a headache. His father sent him home to his mother. As she held him in her arms, he died! She went to the Man of God's room and laid her son on his bed.

She told her husband she needed a young man and a donkey and that she needed to go see the man of God. When he asked what was wrong she responded from her heart, "It is well."

As Elisha saw her coming he sent Gehazi to her. When asked if something was wrong with her son, she responded, "It is well!" When she came to Elisha she caught him by the feet and said, "Did I ask a son of my lord? Did I not say, "Do not deceive me?" Elisha instructed Gehazi to take his staff and go with the woman.

The mother responded, "As the Lord lives, and as your soul lives. I will not leave you. So he arose and followed her." When they returned to her home, he went to his room and life was restored to her son.

An amazing testimony of a woman who did not lose her confidence in God and endured to the end to receive her promise. Her answers to the man of God indicate that she had battled through her disappointments, she had found a place of peace and contentment and *one day* she saw the man of God! How long had he been walking by her house? We don't know, but when you are frustrated with life it clouds your vision and you can't see clearly. I think when she finally came to that place of peace she had clear vision and saw the man of God who had the answer to her heart's desire.

Jesus understood that we needed peace in this world. John 14:27 says, " Peace I leave with you, My peace I give to you; not as the world gives do I give to you. Let not your heart be troubled, neither let it be afraid." My peace I give to you! Have you received this gift?

In this world we think we need food, clothing, house, money in the bank, but our real need is peace of mind. Jesus also told us the Kingdom of God was within and Romans 14:17 says, "For the kingdom of God is not eating and drinking, but righteousness and peace and joy in the Holy Spirit."

God knows we need things and He has told us how to get things. Matthew 6:33 says, "But seek first the kingdom of God and His righteousness and all these things shall be added to you." When God gives us things He adds no sorrow. "The blessing of the Lord makes *one* rich, and He adds no sorrow with it" (Proverbs 10:22).

We live in a sight and sound world where the marketing world knows how to tempt us with the greatest new styles and all the "things" that are supposed to make life better. The problem is we usually end up in debt and struggle to make ends meet. The abundant life Jesus promised is righteousness, peace and joy in the Holy Spirit.

The Shunammite woman grew in confidence in God as she came to the understanding that God loved her, He was not against her and that He would help her in her time of need. This confidence gave her the courage to endure.

When she said, "it is well," her heart was speaking what she knew in her spirit. She understood that the power of life and death was in her words. She would not let go of the promise of God and she would not allow doubt and unbelief in her head.

In 2 Kings 8:1-6 she had another encounter with Elisha. He warns her that a famine is coming to the land for seven years. So she took her household to dwell in the land of the Philistines for 7 years. Upon her return she went to the King to appeal for her house and for her land. There is no mention of her husband traveling with her.

Elisha's servant was setting with the King and the King had asked him to share the great testimonies of Elisha. As he was sharing about a young boy being restored to life, the mother just happened to appear before them. Gehazi was amazed and told the King, this is the woman and her son! The King appointed a certain officer for her saying, "Restore all that was hers, and all the proceeds of the field from the day that she left the land until now."

It all happened one day as the Lord was directing her steps. She was content in her life and she could see and hear the man of God. Paul said, "I have learned in whatever state I am, to be content" (Philippians 4:11). He wrote this is prison!

- Contentment does not mean you have no problems.
- Contentment does not mean you won't be tempted.
- Contentment is the fruit of righteousness.
- Contentment is growing in the grace and knowledge of God.
- Contentment is walking in the peace of God.

As I have mentioned before, time is our most valuable asset. Investing a small amount of time over time brings increase in areas that matter most! You don't have to read the Bible in one day. A verse a day will make a big difference over time.

- Investing small amounts of time over time in God's Word builds faith.
- Investing small amounts of time over time in God's Word builds strength.
- Investing small amounts of time over time in God's Word builds character.

Character will sustain your gift, gives you endurance to wait for the promise and brings contentment to your life. *Contentment is living in faith.*

It will happen one day! No matter how long it takes to get there.

The one thing I know after walking 40 years with God, He is faithful. Stewardship of my heart is my primary responsibility.

"A man is not established by wickedness,
But the root of the righteous cannot be moved."
Proverbs 12:3

Points to Ponder:

- Meditation brings revelation.
- All Kingdom issues are heart issues.
- Our purpose in life is to know Him and the power of His resurrection.
- Praying in the Spirit helps keep our focus on our heavenly home.
- Praying in the Spirit edifies and brings peace to our life.
- It will happen one day, no matter how long it takes to get there!

Don't dig up with doubt, what you planted in faith.

Chapter 8

Bloom Where You Are Planted

He shall be like a tree planted by the rivers of water, that brings forth its fruit in its season, whose leaf also shall not wither; and whatever he does shall prosper.
Psalm 1:3

You have to be planted to bloom! The same faith that brought salvation to your life also empowers you to live a supernatural lifestyle. I'm not talking about a few faith incidents throughout your life, but a sustained lifestyle of moving mountains, breaking addictive behavior, walking through what appears like an impossible situation and bringing the Kingdom of God to earth. This is a normal lifestyle for the child of God. This does not happen overnight. It takes a commitment to God and His Word.

God's Word is your strength! You must walk on the water of His Word and trust in His promises more than what you can see and hear in the natural world. *Living by faith is living by faith in His Word.* This comes from the revelation of His Word that is firmly planted in your spirit. This requires diligence, time and endurance.

You must be planted firmly in the Word of God so that you are not blown about by every wind of doctrine. "Then we will no longer be infants, tossed back and forth by the waves, and blown here and there by every wind of teaching and by the cunning and craftiness of people in their deceitful scheming" (Ephesians 4:14 NIV).

Rose seed germination may take anywhere from a few weeks to a few years, depending on the care of proper feeding, watering and pruning. Yes, pruning. That is one subject we haven't talked about, but is necessary in the cycle of life for the rose and for you and me. "He cuts off every branch of mine that doesn't produce fruit, and he prunes the branches that do bear fruit so they will produce even more" (John 15:2 NLT).

I had been away from our home for several weeks, and when I returned I was shocked to see my rosebushes. They had been pruned, and my husband tried to explain to me it was for the good of the rose. It was really hard for me to believe looking at that ugly little thorn bush. But when spring was beginning, I could see the little buds coming and then the beautiful rose blossomed more beautiful than before! That thorn bush had been transformed into a rose bush!

God in His mercy prunes away the branches that are growing in the wrong direction. He also prunes away branches that are blocking out the 'Son' light that is needed for buds to form. Sometimes our flesh sprouts, and if left unpruned, will drain the strength of our spirit and eventually destroy our effectiveness for the Kingdom of God. You must determine to stay connected to the vine (Jesus) so that you can produce an abundance of fruit. Blooms in our life are expressed as we walk in the joy and peace of the Lord displaying a healthy, vibrant, intimate walk with the Lord.

Our walk in the garden of our life takes a lifetime of learning and growing and will not stop until we are walking with the Master Gardner in His Garden of Life.

During one of my pruning seasons, I was pouting, feeling sorry for myself, when the Lord whispered to my heart, "You need to find the rhythm of life." I began to ponder these words to understand what the Lord was saying. There is always more, and if we want to know what it is, we have to go after it by pondering what He said and asking the Holy Spirit to reveal the truth to us.

I was led to the scripture in 1 Thessalonians 5:23 (KJV): "And the very God of peace sanctify you wholly; and I pray God your whole spirit and soul and body be preserved blameless unto the coming of our Lord Jesus Christ."

As I read this scripture, I realized it wasn't just about my spirit. I had to keep my spirit, soul and body blameless. Each part is created to flow together in "rhythm" so we will not stumble and fall in life.

It is hard to get out of bed a little early to read the Bible and have some quiet time when you are totally exhausted because you have not taken care of your body, have not exercised, eaten a healthy diet and are stressed out over money. It is also hard to be a positive influence on your family and friends when you are discouraged, depressed and disappointed – a reflection of an unhealthy soul.

Outside the Word of God, man is looked at as a two-part creature. The Word of God clearly shows us that we are created in His image, and we are a three-part being: spirit, soul and body.

When we understand the truth of the total man, we can get to the core of human problems. When you are born again, it is your spirit that becomes a new creation! (2 Corinthians 5:17). You have access to two worlds, and the Kingdom of Heaven which you have been born into is superior to the natural world in which you live. "May God's peace and mercy be upon all who live by this principle; they are the new people of God" (Galatians 6:16 NLT). We must learn to walk in our new creation life!

When we understand the truth of the total man, we can get to the core of human problems.

God has created man to live by his spirit and not by his soul: his mind, will and emotions. It is possible to be born again with your spirit alive, yet live in the soulish realm of the Adamic nature.

Conversion gives you the ability to "see" (John 3:3). Your soul changes as you renew your mind. Your body comes into line as you surrender it to the Lord. Romans 12:1-2 (NLT) instructs us what we are to do with the body and soul. "And so, dear brothers and sisters, I plead with you to give your bodies to God because of all he has done for you. Let them be a living and holy sacrifice—the kind he will find acceptable. This is truly the way to worship him. Don't copy the behavior and customs of this world, but let God transform you into a new person by changing the way you think. Then you will learn to know God's will for you, which is good and pleasing and perfect."

Without a yielded heart (spirit), a renewed mind and a surrendered body, we will never understand how to walk in the Spirit and be led by the Spirit. God is focused in bringing our hearts (spirit), minds and bodies in line with His Word and His purpose, which will give us the strength to face the persecution and opposition we face in this world.

The scripture said that your whole spirit, your whole soul and your whole body must be preserved blameless unto the coming of the Lord. Understanding spirit, soul and body unlocks the mystery of the spirit realm so you can hear His voice and be led by the Holy Spirit.

If you don't understand the rhythm of life of the spirit, soul and body you will be confused, frustrated and discouraged. Your spirit was totally changed when you received Jesus as your Lord and Savior. Your body and soul are both impacted by what happened, but the change is not total or complete.

The Holy Spirit that is within you knows all things (1 John 2:20). Only as your mind is renewed will the treasure house of your spirit be released. Third John 2 tells us, "Beloved, I pray that you may prosper in all things and be in health, just as your soul prospers." How are you going to prosper in all things? "As your mind is renewed." Your spiritual growth depends on your priorities in life! I'm still in the process of renewing my mind. I have not arrived, but I have left and I've tasted and seen that the Lord is good!

Your spirit responds to the Holy Spirit when your soul is in agreement with your spirit. Through a renewed mind, your body will follow. Your body doesn't really control anything. It just goes with the flow of what it sees, tastes, hears, smells and feels unless it is influenced by the soul.

Your new life in Christ is about renewing and releasing. After renewing your mind with the Word of God, your soul comes into agreement with what is in your spirit, and revelation knowledge is released so you can experience the benefits of the Kingdom of God.

Your soul is a key that unlocks the door to your spirit and body. The soul contains the mind, will and emotions, all very powerful and must be brought into alignment with the Word of God. The three areas of the soul help the body to know what to do, when to do it and how to do it. God joined the body and soul together with His breath. He breathed into Adam and made the mind, emotions and will with the flesh come alive.

In the new creation life, man is a spirit; he has a soul and lives in a body. Your body is a treasure. "But we have this treasure in earthen vessels, that the excellency of the power may be of God and not of us" (2 Corinthians 4:7).

Your body is a temple, a worship center for God. "Do you not know that your bodies are temples of the Holy Spirit, who is in you, whom you have received from God? You are not your own" (1 Corinthians 6:19 NIV).

Your body is made in the image of God, and the devil hates it. He desires to make your body sick, bring pain to it and premature death. Your body can be made blameless in Christ.

Remember, "But you belong to God, my dear children. You have already won a victory over those people, because the Spirit who lives in you is greater than the spirit who lives in the world" (1 John 4:4 NLT).

There is so much to learn about how we function in this world as a new creation being: spirit, soul and body. I know from personal experience how important it is that you understand the rhythm of life and learn to flow with the Holy Spirit. This totally changed my life from constant confusion and discouragement to understanding how I was created to function in this new creation life.

When I was born again, I had a deep hunger to know God. Like everyone, I had people in my life that I did not like; they had done me wrong, and I didn't want to have anything to do with them!

I kept hearing about the God of love and that I was supposed to love everybody and be a light for Jesus, but I still held hate against a certain person. I just could not figure out what was wrong. If I was supposed to have all this love, why did I still feel this way?

Then, attending a seminar I heard the message about spirit, soul and body; about spiritual warfare and that I had to fight the good fight of faith! The teacher began to teach on 2 Corinthians 10:3-5, and I began to understand how I had to pull down strongholds and cast down imaginations. "For though we walk in the flesh, we do not war according to the flesh. For the weapons of our warfare *are* not carnal but mighty in God for pulling down strongholds, casting down arguments and every high thing that exalts itself against the knowledge of

God, bringing every thought into captivity to the obedience of Christ" (2 Corinthians 10:3-5).

It was not easy, and very honestly at the time, I didn't want to forgive her. She didn't deserve it! Over time as I continued to grow, it was a glorious day when I was able to release all the unforgiveness and bitterness that had grown over several years. It was a fight and satan continued to try and bring things to my remembrance about the hurtful situation. Remember, 1 John 1:9 says He forgives and cleanses. Don't allow the enemy to bring guilt and condemnation against you. You were forgiven instantly, but the cleansing takes time.

I urge you to study this subject. I have studied it for twenty-five years and continually keep this in my heart to learn more and more. Lester Sumrall has a book, *Spirit, Soul and Body; United in Oneness with God.* I highly recommend this book. After twenty-five years, every time I pick it up I receive more and more revelation about my oneness with God.

I love studying the men and women in the Bible. It gives me hope and encouragement. They had great victories and did great exploits for God, but they went through the fire first.

Daniel 11:32b tells us, "But the people who know their God shall be strong, and carry out *great exploits."* Daniel was also in captivity and thrown in a lions' den! Do you want to know his secret? Daniel had an excellent spirit (Daniel 5:12). He guarded his heart above all else!

Remember David? God said he was a man after His own heart! (Acts 13:22). Were these men perfect? Did they ever have a bad thought in their head? Read the Psalms. David poured out his heart. He told just how bad things were, but he always ended by thanking God and rejoicing in His faithfulness.

Sometimes we are our own worst enemy. You are human, you are not perfect and you will make mistakes. When your heart is right, you know instantly when you have messed up and made a mistake. Repent! I have learned to repent fast; I don't give the enemy a chance to form a stronghold in my mind.

We see Esther, a beautiful woman, living in the palace with all the benefits. The road to the palace was filled with sadness. As an orphaned girl, I'm sure there were many lonely days filled with despair.

A unique feature of the book of Esther is that the name of God is not mentioned, but the imprint of God and His ways are obvious throughout this book of the Bible. Esther and Mordecai were two of the most unlikely people to be chosen to play major roles in shaping a nation. He was a Benjamite exile, and she was an adopted orphaned cousin.

Esther had been brought to the palace during a period of time when the King was seeking a new Queen. She had been chosen and was favored by the King.

She lived in the best: home, food, beauty treatments and had favor with everyone in the palace. Trusting Mordecai, she had not revealed that she was a Jew.

Having no idea of her destiny to help bring deliverance to her people, God was equipping Esther for her purpose in life. As an orphan slave girl, she had to learn to be Queen. A person with a slave mentality cannot bring freedom to others.

Esther went from a slave girl to a woman of authority. When she entered a room, she wore her royal robes. They were not only beautiful, but they were indicative of her position as Queen.

Esther received a message from Mordecai about trouble in the country regarding the Jews. Mordecai requested her to go in to the King on behalf of her people. Esther sent word to him reminding him of the protocol to see the King. No one went without a request from the King, and she had not been called for thirty days. Anyone going into the King's inner court would be put to death unless he held out his golden sceptre.

We can see that Esther did not jump at the chance to go in. She had lived in the palace five years, and I believe she had become accustomed to the lifestyle!

Mordecai sent word back to Esther: "Do not think in your heart that you will escape in the king's palace any more than all the other Jews. For if you remain completely silent at this time, relief and deliverance will arise for the Jews from another place, but you and your father's house will perish. Yet who knows whether you have come to the kingdom for *such* a time as this?" (Esther 4:13-14).

Strong words! This was a wake-up call to Esther. She had been brought up in the ways of the Lord, and she understood her people and what was happening. She was stirred in her heart for her people, and she knew what had to be done.

She also knew whatever she would do required wisdom, and she called on the source of her wisdom. She sent word to Mordecai, "Go, gather all the Jews who are present in Shushan, and fast for me; neither eat nor drink for three days, night or day. My maids and I will fast likewise. And so I will go to the king, which *is* against the law; and if I perish, I perish!" (Esther 4:16).

Esther did not panic. She was clothed with the peace of God as she entered the inner courts and she found favor. "And the king said to her, 'What do you wish, Queen Esther? What *is* your request? It shall be given to you – up to half the kingdom!'" (Esther 5:3).

The amazing thing was, Esther asked the King and Haman to a banquet. This had to be God! She had the opportunity to tell the King everything and request his help. They came to the banquet and amazingly she invited them to another meal. She was responding from the peace of God that was in her heart. God had everything in control, and Esther had learned to be still and know God was working all things together for good. Unknown to Esther, everything was not set in place for God's purpose; He needed just a little more time.

That night the King could not sleep and called for the book of the records of the Chronicles be read to him. It was brought to light that Mordecai had protected the King from danger and had not been honored for it.

The next day at the second banquet, Haman was exposed and was hung on the gallows that he had prepared for Mordecai's death! Esther's request for the Jews was granted. Please read the book of Esther; it is a wonderful testimony of God's timing and His faithfulness to all who serve Him.

Just as Esther was brought to the Kingdom for such a time as this, you also have a divine purpose for the Kingdom of God. Esther learned to be a Queen and accepted her responsibilities in the Kingdom.

You are the daughter of the King of Kings! A child of God. You have all the forces and resources of Heaven behind you.

When Esther entered a room with her royal robe on, everyone knew who she was. As a woman of God, you are clothed with the robe of righteousness. When you walk in a room, people should know there is something different about you. Your robe of righteousness gives you the authority to infiltrate the powers of darkness that are trying to kill, steal and destroy your family, finances, your health and relationships.

The Master Designer has created a set of clothes for the woman of God that is worry and fear-free that will never wear out. They are designed with you in mind. You are an original, a unique woman of God. There are no copies of His original design for you, but we all share the common thread of forgiveness given to us by Jesus Christ.

You have been clothed with the garment of salvation, the robe of righteousness and the garment of praise. "I will greatly rejoice in the Lord, my soul shall be joyful in my God; for He has clothed me with the garments of salvation, He has covered me with the robe of righteousness . . ." (Isaiah 61:10). ". . . The garment of praise for the spirit of heaviness . . ." (Isaiah 61:3).

Your robe of righteousness gives you your identity as a woman of God. "Righteousness" is a big word, which simply means "in right standing with God." You accepted Jesus Christ and now you are in right standing with God. You are free to worship the Lord with your garment of praise! Wrap your garment of praise around your robe of righteousness, and leave no opening for the fiery darts of the enemy to penetrate your robe. Your garment of praise will stop the disappointments and discouragements that try to rip your robe.

Guard your wardrobe; don't get caught naked and ashamed. ". . . Blessed (happy, to be envied) is he who stays awake (alert) and who guards his clothes, so that he may not be naked and [have the shame of being] seen exposed!" (Revelation 16:15 AMPC).

In the Garden when Eve listened to the enemy, her covering was torn, and a fiery dart of deception took root. She found herself naked and ashamed and tried to cover her sin with fig leaves. In our hurt and pain, we sometimes cover our unforgiveness, not allowing the scarlet thread of forgiveness to wash our robe of righteousness.

What condition is your robe in? As you walk the runway of life with all its detours, has your robe had a few tears and rips from jealously, competition, fear and worry causing you to stumble over the loose threads of your life? You must learn to take the threads of each day and allow God to weave them together for His masterpiece.

I have good news for you. No matter what shape your robe is in, if you have totally unraveled or just have a few loose edges, all you have to do is submit the threads to the Lord. He will take the loose ends of your life and weave your life into the original design He created just for you!

Designer clothes for the woman of God give you the authority to infiltrate the powers of darkness that are trying to kill, steal and destroy your family, finances, relationships and health. They also give you the ability to be free of guilt, condemnation, fear and inferiority. You can walk the runway of life with the joy of the Lord as your strength, holding your head high in garments created by the Master Designer, Jesus Christ!

You might not understand why you are in the place where you are. You may have to learn to tolerate something that you do not like to eventually get to where you want to be. Like the flower that bloomed through the concrete crack on my patio, we have to make the best of our situation and bloom where we have been planted.

Every chapter in your life builds a foundation for the next chapter. Your purpose in life is not determined by your current circumstances. God could be protecting you from a situation you know nothing about. His timing is always perfect, and He only has the best for you. Hebrews 10:35-36 tells us, "Therefore do not cast away your confidence, which has great reward. For you have need of endurance, so that after you have done the will of God, you may receive the promise."

When I graduated from Bible school, I thought the world was waiting for me. I knew that God had called me to teach His Word, and I had many prophetic words confirming this.

I lived in Tulsa and the City of Faith Hospital had just been opened. I had worked in hospital administration before going to Bible school, and as I drove by the hospital I had the thought I should stop and go in. I refused to follow up on this thought! There was no way I was going to return to a hospital to work. I was "called" to teach God's Word.

After about six months, a woman I greatly admired and who was known for her prophetic ministry, said to me, "Joyce, do you work in a hospital?" "No!" I responded. She said, "When I look at you I see you in a hospital setting." I finally gave in and went to the hospital. After talking to a woman, she said, "Where have you been for the last six months? You have the qualifications for a position we need to fill."

I took the job, but I didn't have a good attitude about it. Little by little, as the Lord worked on my attitude, I settled in and enjoyed my work. One day sitting at my desk the Lord spoke to me, "You can leave now." "Leave? Where am I going?" "Didn't I tell you that you would travel the world?" Well, I got out some paper and put it in my typewriter (yes, a typewriter) and started typing my resignation letter.

Six months later, with my family, we were living in Scotland; and I had no idea it would be for twelve years and that I would travel throughout Europe and Asia from there.

You have to learn to bloom where you are planted. If you find yourself planted under some concrete, look for the crack to find your way out!

"For as the earth brings forth its bud, as
the garden causes
the things that are sown in it to spring
forth, so the
Lord God will cause righteousness and praise
to spring forth before all nations"
Isaiah 61:1

Points to Ponder

- When we understand the truth of the total man, we can get to the core of human problems.
- Living by faith is living by faith in His Word.
- God has clothed you with the robe of righteousness, you can walk boldly into the throne room of God and ask for help in your time of need.
- Your garment of praise surrounds your robe of righteousness and keeps the fiery darts of the enemy from penetrating into your life.
- Your Designer clothes give you the authority to infiltrate the powers of darkness.

You take care of the sowing;
God will take care of the growing!

Chapter 9

Reaping the Harvest

"Finally, my brethren, be strong in the Lord and in the power of His might."
Ephesians 6:10

We have plowed the ground, planted the seeds, cultivated the weeds, fertilized and pruned the plants. Now we must guard the plants from destruction and disease so we can reap the harvest.

When I visited a botanical garden I found everything in it was beautiful! The garden was protected from outside predators' attacks. The environment was created and perfectly maintained for the plants to grow and mature into their natural state of beauty.

We have to purposely create an environment to protect the garden of our heart. Your heart is the primary target for the enemy. If we choose not to align our life with God's truth, we leave our heart exposed where satan has a clear shot for a fiery dart to pierce our heart.

While we were away for several weeks one time, I forgot to get rid of some cut roses in water on the dining room table before leaving. When we returned the flowers were dead, but insects were flying all around the swamp created by the water.

I had not invited them into our home, but the environment was just right and they invited themselves. The environment I created unintentionally was the invitation. I don't know if you have ever had to fight any of these little creatures, but it seemed like they multiplied faster than we could get rid of them!

Every day, twenty-four hours a day, your enemy is seeking whom he may devour. "Stay alert! Watch out for your great enemy, the devil. He prowls around like a roaring lion, looking for someone to devour" (1 Peter 5:8 NLT). A very real enemy has been strategizing against you; coming against your emotions, your mind, your family, your finances and your future.

Many people will say to me, "I am under attack." I always ask them if they are born again. If you are born again, you are living in a war zone You are living in a spiritual battle fighting for your life. As you grow in the knowledge of God's Word, you will become aware of the strategies of the enemy and discern the spirits that are coming against you; and understand you have been given the authority to stop the enemy in his tracks!

The effects of this war in the invisible world are revealed in depression, discouragement, emotional instability and mental fatigue.

Being a child of God doesn't give you immunity from the assaults of the enemy, but it does give you access to the Kingdom of Heaven and to the power of the Holy Spirit.

The people around you are not your enemy! Situations that come into your life in the physical are not your problem. The devil that is prowling around wants you ignorant of the spiritual realities behind the physical challenges. Things you perceive with your physical senses are not the real issues. Your enemy, the devil, may be invisible, but he is real and very persistent in his purpose to kill, steal and destroy.

You have to have an understanding firmly planted in your heart that there are two worlds: the physical and the spiritual. When you were born again, the eyes of your understanding were opened to the spiritual world. God is a spirit, you are a spirit and the devil is a spirit.

First Corinthians 15:44-49 NIV tells us, "It is sown a natural body, it is raised a spiritual body. If there is a natural body, there is also a spiritual body. So it is written: 'The first man Adam became a living being'; the last Adam, a life-giving spirit. The spiritual did not come first, but the natural, and after that the spiritual. The first man was of the dust of the earth; the second man is of heaven. As was the earthly man, so are those who are of the earth; and as is the heavenly man, so also are those who are of heaven. And just as we have borne the image of the earthly man, so shall we bear the image of the heavenly man."

As I have said before, we live in a sight and sound world and in the midst of all the frustration of the world we live in, it is very easy to lose sight of the real battle. That is why we must create an environment around us to protect us from the enemy and invite the power of Heaven into our life.

As we studied in the previous chapter, God clothed you with the garments of salvation: your robe of righteousness and a garment of praise. You were also given a full set of armor to protect your garments of salvation in this world, but you have to put on your armor.

In growing roses you have to create the right environment for all of your work in preparing the ground and planting seeds to be able to bear fruit and reap a harvest. The same is true in your spiritual life. You can sow the seeds, but if the environment is not right the seeds will fall by the wayside.

Paul wrote the book of Ephesians to a group of believers who were rich with spiritual blessings, but living as beggars because they were ignorant of their spiritual wealth. Paul gives us a place to start; a prayer for spiritual vision, asking the Lord to open our eyes and give us a spirit of wisdom and revelation in the knowledge of the Lord and that our understanding be enlightened (Ephesians 1:17-23).

Paul confirms our position in heavenly places and gives instruction to our daily life ending with our battle gear for victory. The battle gear revealed to you by the Holy Spirit is part of your daily walk with the Lord. It is not something for you to put on and take off. The devil does not knock on your door and say, "I'm going to attack you today."

Satan knows he cannot defeat you if you are truly born again and have the Holy Spirit residing within you, but he can make your life miserable on this earth. Jesus came to destroy the works of the enemy. First John 3:8 says, "For this purpose the Son of God was manifested, that He might destroy the works of the devil." You have to enforce this victory in your personal life, and you have been given all the tools you need to do it.

Ephesians 6:10-18 NIV states:

"Finally, be strong in the Lord and in his mighty power. Put on the full armor of God, so that you can take your stand against the devil's schemes. For our struggle is not against flesh and blood, but against the rulers, against the authorities, against the powers of this dark world and against the spiritual forces of evil in the heavenly realms. Therefore put on the full armor of God, so that when the day of evil comes, you may be able to stand your ground, and after you have done everything, to stand. Stand firm then, with the belt of truth buckled around your waist, with the breastplate of righteousness in place, And with your feet fitted with the readiness that comes from the gospel of peace. In addition to all this, take up the shield of faith, with which you can extinguish all the flaming arrows of the evil one. Take the helmet of salvation and the sword of the Spirit, which is the word of God. And pray in the Spirit on all occasions with all kinds of prayers and requests. With this in mind, be alert and always keep on praying for all the Lord's people."

Today many churches have allowed the world into their church by becoming seeker friendly and have become lethargic and lazy in the battle, and this works for satan's advantage.

He beats you down with discontentment and discouragement. Makes you believe your situation will never change, and places a burden of shame and guilt that is too heavy to carry. Your spiritual armor has become tarnished, and he has you where he wants you.

Today is a new day! It is time to draw the battle line and say, "No more, devil." It is time to polish your armor and fight the good fight of faith. Together we can do this. We need each other in this battle, encouraging each other in our walk with God. You are not alone; your Father has you in His heart, and He wants to be in your heart.

> *Today is a new day! It is time to draw the battle line and say, "No more, devil."*

Paul tells us where our strength comes from. He exhorts us to be strong in the Lord and in His mighty power so that we can stand against the devil's schemes. The devil has only one scheme to use on you, deception. Deception always has a smidgen of truth. Your only protection against deception is to know the truth! Truth exposes deception.

Paul also reminds us where the battle is taking place: against the spiritual forces of evil in the heavenly realms. Only the weapons that God reveals to us by the Spirit are effective in the heavenly places. We must set our minds on things above, pulling from our heavenly home.

We are not just walking through this world trying to make it to the rapture. I was raised on "I'll Fly Away." Every Sunday dear sweet Sister Emma graced us with this song. As a girl, I sat there every Sunday fully expecting to see her fly away!

Many Christians have an escape mentality: "Push the rapture button; I want out of here!" No! Ephesians 2:6 NIV says, "And God raised us up with Christ and seated us with him in the heavenly realms in Christ Jesus."

Yes, we are still on earth living through the turmoil of life: disease, destruction and hardships, but through our position in Christ, we always walk in hope, and hope does not disappoint. Hope has a name! Jesus.

The best the enemy can do to you is make you insecure, fearful and unable to enjoy your inheritance in Christ. He cannot unseat you, but he can intimidate you and render you ineffective for the Kingdom of God on earth.

Paul tells us twice to put on the "full" armor of God (Ephesians 6:11,13). Each piece has a specific place on your body and a specific purpose for your protection against the enemy.

Paul starts with the belt of truth buckled around our waist. Truth becomes your starting place and gives you the strength to face the enemy and to stand in the face of discouragement and speak words of truth to bring your enemy down! Just like Jesus spoke, "It is written!"

Truth holds all things together, so the belt of truth wrapped around you gives stability and helps you keep your balance as you take your stand. We will not get caught off guard by the enemy when we have the belt of truth secured. Another purpose for your belt is to help keep other parts of your armor in place.

The belt of truth holds your breastplate of righteousness in place, which is covering your heart. The theme carried throughout this book is about guarding your heart. Above all else!

Your heart is the source of life in the natural and in the supernatural. Righteous living is not about being perfect. Righteous living is when your spirit (heart) is submitted to

God, your mind is being renewed and your body is yielded to the Holy Spirit to receive teaching, correction and training in righteousness (2 Timothy 3:16).

The enemy knows that if you don't see yourself completely forgiven, firmly anchored in the righteousness of God through Christ Jesus, you will not use your breastplate to stop the fiery darts of the enemy.

We put on the breastplate of righteousness by making a conscious effort to renew our mind. This is not a once in a lifetime action; it is day by day, hour by hour, a repeated choice as you face the temptations of life and fight against jealousy and pride, lust, addictive habits and greed.

You can't just show up at church on Sunday and live like the devil all week. Putting on your best Sunday dress, lifting your hands in praise, then go home to have roasted pastor for lunch. When you allow attitudes that don't line up with the Word of God, you are creating an unrighteous environment that attracts darkness and will destroy your root system. Righteous living, a life grounded and rooted in the love of God, will always expose the enemy.

Living in a dark world is not easy, but the rewards are out of this world! God knows where we are and will lead us by the still waters. As I shared before, when I had really messed up, I was crying out to God to forgive me and help me. He spoke, "When your heart is right, I will bless your ignorance." I have leaned into this word so many times it is plastered to my heart!

Stop trying to be perfect. That is impossible for you to do and will drive you crazy! Remember, God is working in you

(Philippians 2:13). As you feed on the Word of God, the grace of God is releasing the power within you to change the things that you cannot do on your own. He is realigning your passions and attitudes and giving you the strength to live in a way that is pleasing to Him and is a blessing to others.

You give the devil free access when you are not aligning your life with the Word of God. Not being perfect, but having a heart attitude to know Him and the power of His resurrection. God looks on the heart.

When Jesus was asked by the Pharisees when the Kingdom of God would come, He answered, "The kingdom of God does not come with observation" (Luke17:20). He reminded them of the days of Noah and Lot. In verse 32, Jesus says, "Remember Lot's wife." She was leaving the city, but her heart was still in the city. She suffered the consequences.

Her feet were not shod with the gospel of peace, and she walked into the trap of the enemy.

Jesus understood our need for peace in this world as He told us in John 14:27, "Peace I leave with you, My peace I give to you; not as the world gives do I give to you. Let not your heart be troubled, neither let it be afraid." Jesus leaves the disciples with a gift of peace. He repeats this with the emphasis of "My" peace as an impartation to them.

"Not as the world gives do I give to you." Not material possessions as the world gives, but the peace that passes all understanding and guides your footsteps into all truth.

Satan also knows the power of peace, and that is why he stirs up discord and division. He is the king of chaos and confusion, looking for any opportunity to nibble at your peace.

A life without peace is totally unprotected from the darts of the enemy. Your vision becomes clouded, and you cannot hear God's voice in the midst of the chaos. Tension flows throughout your relationships and home, causing division and opens the door for deception.

If your breastplate of righteousness is not firmly placed over your heart, there is no peace. If you don't have peace with God, you will never know the peace of God.

Understanding that you are in right standing with God through the shed blood of Christ Jesus is what causes you to walk in peace and keeps your mind on Him. "You will keep him in perfect peace, whose mind is stayed on You, because he trusts in You" (Isaiah 26:3).

Peace is a divine gift imparted to the child of God. It is your responsibility to nurture this gift in your daily walk. Peace will guard your heart and also guide you into the plans and purposes that God has for you. When your feet are shod with the gospel of peace, you are always ready to follow the light He shines on your path.

How do you activate the peace in your heart? "Let the peace of Christ rule in your hearts, since as members of one body you were called to peace. And be thankful" (Colossians 3:15 NIV). "Be anxious for nothing, but in everything by prayer and supplication, with thanksgiving, let your requests be made known to God; and the peace of God, which surpasses all understanding, will guard your hearts and minds through Christ Jesus" (Philippians 4:6-7).

The key, "with thanksgiving." When God hears a faith-filled prayer from a grateful heart, His light of peace shines on us. Our emotions are stabilized, our sharp tongue is cooled and our footsteps are walking in the center of His will.

Faith in God's Word leads to thankfulness which activates peace in our heart, preparing our feet with the gospel of peace. Our feet are ready to march on and conquer the mountain before us! *"As you therefore have received Christ Jesus the Lord, so walk in Him" (Colossians 2:6).*

We have our shield of faith ready to stop any fiery dart the enemy shoots our way!

I have heard much teaching in my life about faith, and I'm sure you have also. After all, "Without faith it is impossible to please Him, for he who comes to God must believe that He is, and that He is a rewarder of those who diligently seek Him" (Hebrews 11:6).

We come to Jesus by having faith in His Word, believing in our heart and confessing with our mouth (Romans 10:9-10). By the power of your words you were delivered from the kingdom of darkness into the Kingdom of Light. "Death and life are in the power of the tongue, and those who love it will eat its fruit" (Proverbs 18:21). Proverbs is full of scriptures regarding the tongue.

"The spirit of a man will sustain him in sickness, but who can bear a broken spirit?" (Proverbs 18:14).

"The spirit of a man is the lamp of the Lord . . ." (Proverbs 20:27). When the light of the gospel is lost, you can no longer see to follow the Lord.

"A cheerful heart is good medicine, but a crushed spirit dries up the bones" (Proverbs 17:22 NIV).

How is a spirit crushed and broken? Psalm 64:2-3 tells us,

"Hide me from the secret plots of the wicked, from the rebellion of the workers of iniquity, who sharpen their tongue like a sword, and bend *their bows to shoot* their arrows – bitter words."

Bitter words can drain the life out of your spirit. If you don't understand that you have the authority to stop them, they will steal your vision and destroy the gift that is within you. That is the ploy of the enemy, to make you dysfunctional with disappointment and discouragement.

Jesus tells us in Matthew 12:35, "A good man out of the good treasure of his heart brings forth good things, and an evil man out of the evil treasure brings forth evil things." Words transfer faith or fear.

The world is full of hate, and when hate-filled words come against you, they can destroy you unless you know you have the power to stop them.

The old saying, "Sticks and stones may break my bones, but words will never hurt me," comes from the pit of hell! Words are the only thing that can crush and break your spirit. I'm sure we have all felt the sting of words spoken in bitterness or anger. You've heard it said, "It's not what they said, but how they said it."

Words contain power, and the condition of your heart determines the effect of those words. Words can build you up or tear you down. There is a definite link between your heart and your words. "Let the words of my mouth and the meditation of my heart be acceptable in Your sight, O Lord, my strength and my Redeemer" (Psalm 19:14).

When we were living in Scotland, God led me to a certain area to teach Bible studies, and soon afterwards moved us to this area to start a church. Little did I know I had just been put on the front lines.

When I went to my first Bible study, as I was ringing the doorbell, the Lord whispered in my ear, "There is an enemy in the camp." My first thought was, "I have to get out of here," but before I could turn and run, the door opened and I knew my enemy. Unknown to me, as everyone was leaving the Bible study, the enemy spoke to each person, saying, "She is a false prophet."

I soon began to feel the effects of her bitter words being spoken, not just in that area, but throughout Scotland. I began to become weary and wanted to get out. I begged my husband to get me out, take me back to the states. After several months of this, I received a call from a dear friend, Beth Alves. When I answered the phone, she said, "Joyce, do you know someone in that town is trying to kill you!" I said, "Yes." She said, "If you don't do something about it, she is going to do it!"

I said, "I don't know what to do," and she said, "You have authority. Use it!" and she hung up. Wow! What a phone call! When I heard her voice, I had expected comfort, but instead, I got a kick in the butt.

The next week we received a call from a minister we knew in the states, and he told us he was in Scotland and would like to teach a Bible study in our home. We said yes, and the night I opened the door, he looked directly into my eyes and said, "I will be teaching on Psalm 64." I had no doubt that God had sent him with a Word for me and I determined to listen.

I have studied and meditated on this Psalm from that night on. When I read the first verse, "Hear my voice, O God, in my meditation; preserve my life from fear of the enemy," I said, "Lord, I don't fear her." He said, "You anticipate her words; that is fear in action!" Satan was using her to try to kill the gift of God that was in me to teach the Word. We must constantly remember we are not fighting flesh and blood, but the powers of darkness.

I could feel myself getting stronger in the Lord as I meditated Psalm 64. The Holy Spirit began to bring revelation to me from this Psalm and brought to my remembrance Luke 10:19: "Behold, I give you the authority to trample on serpents and scorpions, and over all the power of the enemy, and nothing shall by any means hurt you."

Every day I said, "I take authority over every curse word spoken against me in the name of Jesus." A curse is a proclamation of harm or a declaration of detriment. I don't know how long it was, but one day I was in my kitchen washing dishes when my daughter entered the room and began to strum her guitar. She was practicing for the worship team. I suddenly felt the presence of the Lord, and I knew my day of deliverance had come.

I said, "Jeni, don't stop." As she continued playing I felt a release. It felt like a band had just been broken from around my head and I was free! This was a two-year period of my life from the night of that first Bible study.

"But God shall shoot at them with an arrow; suddenly they shall be wounded. So He will make them stumble over their own tongue" (Psalm 64:7-8). This is exactly what happened. I had prayed for the person. Honestly, I didn't want to, but as I walked in obedience to the Word of God, He opened my heart towards her. I only saw her one time afterwards while living in Scotland, and I never had the opportunity to speak with her, but I trust God to look over her soul and heal the hurt in her life. When you don't walk in forgiveness, a root of bitterness springs forth, this defiles many.

Did I enjoy this time? No! But my shield of faith was polished and shining bright after this. God immediately turned everything around for good. Not only were there invitations in Scotland, but throughout the nations. I had a voice with a "real life lesson to share"!

Yes, there were more battles and I'm not dead yet, but I am more alert to satan's deceptive ways. I am also stronger in the spirit and the knowledge of the Word of God.

I don't focus on the devil and what he is doing; I know he is bad. I keep my focus on God and His greatness. The real always exposes the counterfeit.

"And the apostles said to the Lord, 'Increase our faith.' So the Lord said, 'If you have faith as a mustard seed, you can say to this mulberry tree, "Be pulled up by the roots and be planted in the sea," and it would obey you'" (Luke 17:5-6). Jesus changed the focus of their faith from its size to its effect. Enduring faith gives strength to your shield and stops the fiery darts of the enemy.

Faith is action. It is adapting your behavior, your decisions and lifestyle to the standards of God's Word. It is choosing to walk in obedience when you can't see the outcome.

Faith speaks. "And since we have the same spirit of faith, according to what is written, 'I believed and therefore I spoke,' we also believe and therefore speak" (2 Corinthians 4:13).

Faith-filled words coming from your mouth will destroy every lie that rises up against you. This act of faith becomes the shield guarding you against the enemy's attack.

Faith-filled words coming from your mouth will destroy every lie that rises up against you.

God has given us armor from our head, with the helmet of salvation, to the soles of our feet, with the preparation of peace. Salvation is about rescue and restoration. God has rescued us from the snare of the enemy and restored to us everything that was lost in the Garden.

I can imagine Paul sitting in prison chained to a Roman soldier. As he studied each piece of his armor, the Lord began to speak to him about the armor of God. As he watched the soldiers prepare for battle, he saw that the helmet was the last defensive armament to be put in place. The helmet was vital for survival, protecting the brain and mind, the command station for the rest of the body. If the head was damaged, the rest of the armor would be of little value.

In the spirit the helmet of salvation gives us hope and protects our soul. Hope is the anchor of our soul. It keeps us steady and does not allow us to become blinded from the knowledge of God. Hope keeps our focus in line. "But since we belong to the day, let us be sober, putting on faith and love as a breastplate, and the hope of salvation as a helmet" (1 Thessalonians 5:8" NIV).

The mind is the battleground. "For the weapons of our warfare *are* not carnal but mighty in God for pulling down strongholds, casting down arguments and every high thing that exalts itself against the knowledge of God, bringing every thought into captivity to the obedience of Christ" (2 Corinthians 10:4-5). Our helmet will stop the strongholds and every thought that tries to exalt itself against the knowledge of God and tries to bring doubt and unbelief into our heart.

The helmet protects our identity as a child of God. The first thing satan tempted Jesus with was His identity: "If you are the Son of God." Jesus understood that His power was in His identity as the Son of God. He recognized the tactic of satan and spoke faith-filled words, "It is written." This is the perfect example of how to use the sword of the Spirit, the Word of God.

The sword of the Spirit is the only weapon of our warfare that we are told specifically what it is: the Word of God.

"For the word of God is living and powerful, and sharper than any two-edged sword, piercing even to the division of soul and spirit, and of joints and marrow, and is a discerner of the thoughts and intents of the heart" (Hebrews 4:12).

The Word of God has the power to discern our thoughts and attitudes that are contrary to God's Word and cut asunder those attitudes and thoughts, bringing them into captivity. That is the Christian battle, and that is how we use the offensive weapon in our armor.

There are two different Greek words referring to the Word of God: *logos* and *rhema. Logos* is the written Word. Through the written Word we can learn about God and know His ways. The *rhema* Word denotes the spoken Word revealed to us by the Holy Spirit, causing faith to spring forth from our mouth. The

Word comes alive and we know and understand the *logos* Word of God. It is that still small voice that brings life.

Logos and *rhema* are both crucial to our Christian life, for God uses the *logos* Word to speak His *rhema* Word to us. The *rhema* Word imparts life to us. "It is the Spirit who gives life; the flesh profits nothing. The words that I speak to you are spirit, and *they* are life" (John 6:63).

As we read and meditate the *logos*, with our hearts open, the Lord will speak *rhema* words to impart life into us. No freshly spoken Word of God is void of power.

As we walk the runway of life and through all the detours, we are being trained and learning to be skillful in the use of our sword. We are told in Hebrews that we must become gradually more knowledgeable and skilled in the Word of God to discern good from evil.

"For though by this time you ought to be teachers, you need someone to teach you again the first principles of the oracles of God; and you have come to need milk and not solid food. For everyone who partakes only of milk is unskilled in the word of righteousness, for he is a babe. But solid food belongs to those who are of full age, that is, those who by reason of use have their senses exercised to discern both good and evil" (Hebrews 5:12-14).

Our spiritual senses must be sharpened by "reason of use" to become skillful with our sword.

As we have put on the armor of God, next Paul tells us, "Praying always with all prayer and supplication in the Spirit, being watchful to this end with all perseverance and supplication for all the saints" (Ephesians 6:18).

Prayer is the glue that keeps us all together as we learn to use our armor. We have done all; now we are standing. While we are standing, we are praying. Standing does not mean we are doing nothing.

Standing does not mean we are doing nothing.

Prayer is the door we open to make our requests known to God. As we have received revelation from the Word of God and know our inheritance, "Let us therefore come boldly to the throne of grace, that we may obtain mercy and find grace to help in time of need" (Hebrews 4:16).

Prayer is having confidence in God giving us the grace to ask according to His will (1 John 5:14-15). First Thessalonians 5:17-18 tells us to "Pray without ceasing, in everything give thanks; for this is the will of God in Christ Jesus for you." Praying without ceasing is always having your heart towards God, walking in humility, knowing that you are nothing without Him.

As I said before the secret of asking is abiding. "If you abide in Me, and My words abide in you, you will ask what you desire, and it shall be done for you" (John 15:7). When you are abiding in His Word, His desire becomes your desire; and asking is an automatic response to receiving the desires of your heart.

Joy is a fruit of the Spirit and Jesus tells us to, ". . . Ask, and you will receive, that your joy may be full" (John 16:24).

During World War II, an officer was briefing his men on how to take a certain objective. He demonstrated to them the manner in which they needed to hug the ground so as to stay below enemy fire. He said in conclusion, "If you advance on your knees, you will always be safe" (Author unknown).

Women of the world manipulate.
Women of God infiltrate on their knees!

Points to Ponder:

- You have to intentionally create an environment that will protect your heart.
- You were clothed with the garments of salvation, but you have to put on the armor of God.
- You have been given authority to stop all the fiery darts of the enemy.
- Righteous living is adapting your lifestyle to the standard of God's Word.
- Prayer is having the confidence to ask.

Chapter 10

From My Heart to Your Heart

"The Lord gives the word [of power]; the women who bear and publish [the news] are a great host."
Psalm 68:11 AMPC

My heart is full of love and joy as I think about you and the potential that is within you. You were created for God's purpose. There is nothing in this world that can satisfy you until you feel His pleasure in your life. We have all been given a lot in life; you either park on it or you build on it.

One thing you must understand is that your walk with God is a personal daily walk. There are no shortcuts. You build your own history with God. Others can encourage you and help you along the way, but ultimately you make the decisions for your life.

God understands human weakness. When you understand it, your weakness becomes your strength as you rely on His grace and mercy in your life.

When we lived in Scotland, one of our favorite places to go was St. Andrews. It is a beautiful town, and we loved the beach there. Part of the movie, "Chariots of Fire," was filmed on this beach. My favorite line of the movie was spoken there by Eric Liddell to his sister, "God made me to run, and when I run I feel His pleasure."

My purpose in life is to know Him and the power of His resurrection, and my goal in life is to feel His pleasure. Your destiny is Heaven. Can I be honest? I get tired of hearing so much talk about destiny. God has my destiny in His hand, and as I fulfil my purpose in life to know Him, then I can trust Him with my destiny. I don't have to work out my destiny. I'm on my way to Heaven shouting Glory!

My purpose in life is to know Him and the power of His resurrection, and my goal in life is to feel His pleasure.

Society today puts a heavy burden on men and women. Men feel the need to perform, women feel the need to conform, but God desires to transform you into the person He created you to be.

When you understand that you are living for one person, it takes the pressure off. You don't live to please others; you live to please Him. As little girls we play "make believe," and this plays right into the hand of the devil. That thinking trains you to live a fantasy life which turns into a nightmare.

In the world we live in, convenience outweighs commitment. The world we live in is designed for instant and disposable. Instant satisfaction, instant money, instant potatoes! We have disposable diapers, disposable razors and disposable people. Many approach marriage with the mind-set, "If it doesn't work, you can dispose of them and get a new one."

There is only one true standard in life: the Word of God. As we build our life on His Word, we find our life and His peace.

This is not a book about a formula for success or a self-help book. This is a book about the heart, God's heart towards you and your heart towards God. I'm simply sharing from my heart some of the truths I have learned from my forty years of walking with the Lord. I'm still learning, moving on toward my destiny with great anticipation of tomorrow.

So, I urge you, dear sister, get your cup of tea, relax and allow the Holy Spirit to hover over you, bringing light to the darkness that would like to swallow your life with the chaos and confusion that bring turmoil to your mind.

"But I fear, lest somehow, as the serpent deceived Eve by his craftiness, so your minds may be corrupted from the simplicity that is in Christ" (2 Corinthians 11:3). The simplicity of the gospel is: Jesus loves me this I know, for the Bible tells me so! If we would get this settled in our hearts, it would change our life.

All women need love and worth to complete their uniqueness. Men and women are redemptively equal, but functionally different. When God made woman, He took from Adam's rib making her equal from something He had already created. Women were made from man in the beginning and since then, man has been made from woman.

God took the nurturing and tenderness of His own nature already breathed into Adam and gave them to woman. Man was left to be the disciplinarian, the tough to guide and lead. As we learn to appreciate and respect the God-given uniqueness of men and women, we will enjoy life.

Am I saying women cannot be leaders? No. Deborah was a woman, gifted by God to be a leader. She had the respect of her countrymen because her life was submitted to God. She had been appointed by God to bring her people back to God, to liberate them from the power of their oppressors. The entire nation acknowledged her as its leader.

Deborah understood that Barak was chosen by God to lead the Army. She did not place herself over him, but next to him working together for God's glory. Deborah's tactful, spiritual leadership freed Barak to carry out the duties assigned to him. He was a man of strength and wisdom and recognized the gift within Deborah. They worked together as two people, man and woman, and carried out God's purpose for their lives.

Through Deborah's understanding of God's way, she remained the leader and was responsible for all the decisions as she watched Barak and his 10,000 men conquer the enemy.

Lydia is another woman leader. She was a businesswoman in a man's world who opened Europe to the Good News of Jesus.

God does not always work according to a set pattern; He is looking for men and women who are willing to be used as instruments in any way He chooses. "And we no longer see each other in our former state, Jew or non-Jew, rich or poor; male or female – because we're all one through our union with Jesus Christ with no distinction between us" (Galatians 3:28 TPT).

Men and women are created to work together with God to fulfill the plan and purpose of God on earth. I call this "the power of we." *God is the power. His Word in us activates the power and brings transformation to the world.*

In closing ... my challenge to you is:

Are you prepared for a divine interruption in your life?

- Have you planted good seeds in the garden of your heart?
- Have you pulled the weeds that drain all the nutrients from your seed?
- Have you used the fertilizer to bring growth in your life, or allowed it to destroy the seeds of your dreams?
- Have you cultivated the soil of your heart so the Holy Spirit can breathe fresh life into your heart?

Mary, the mother of Jesus, had a divine interruption. Zecharias, John the Baptist's father, also had a divine interruption. He questioned Gabriel and tried to tell him why it would not work. He was made mute because he did not believe the words delivered by the angel (Luke 1:19-20).

When the angel appeared to Mary, his first words were, "Do not be afraid, Mary, for you have found favor with God" (Luke 1:30). After the angel announced that she would soon be pregnant, she questioned him with honesty and uncertainty, saying, "How can this be?" (vs. 34). The angel explained to her how the Holy Spirit would overshadow her and the Son of God would be born.

Mary did not doubt the word, but she did not understand the word so she asked questions. She humbly responded, saying, "Let it be to me according to your word" (vs. 38).

After Jesus was born, Simeon prepared Mary for her future. "(Yes, a sword will pierce through your own soul also), that the thoughts of many hearts may be revealed" (Luke 2:35). Mary was beginning to see the whole picture. She wouldn't appear to be blessed, but she knew, "Someday all generations will call me blessed."

God knew that Mary had what it would take to walk through all the difficulties that Jesus' birth would bring into her life. Mary was real; she faced her fear and received the Word of the Lord spoken to her. She would hold her head high in the midst of all the misunderstandings and accusations.

Jesus Himself challenged her at one point. Attending a wedding with His mother and His disciples, the wine ran out. Mary told Jesus about this situation, and He responded, "Woman, what does your concern have to do with Me? My hour has not yet come" (John 2:4). "Woman?" What is this? Not "mother"? She didn't appear to be hurt or take offense as she instructed the servants, "Whatever He says to you, do it" (vs. 5). Evidently Mary felt that He needed a little help getting started.

We read that Mary continually pondered things in her heart; words spoken to her by the angel, words from her cousin Elizabeth, Anna, Simeon and the many people who confirmed the Word of the Lord.

Her faithfulness and obedience took her to the foot of the cross. I am sure her pain of the crucifixion turned to joy as she heard the news, "The grave is empty! He has risen from the dead!"

Remember, each season of your life needs time to grow for the "real" seed to mature. You must water the seed with love and laughter for it to mature to its full potential.

I don't know what season or stage of life you are in, but God created you as one of a kind. Our uniqueness makes us valuable. You have what it takes! Your nature and character were custom designed just for you. Recognizing this truth will give you the confidence in your relationship with God, where all things are possible.

We all go through the stripping process of taking off the old and putting on the new. You will not be disappointed with what you find. You can't go back to the very beginning, but you can start now and make a new ending! Passing over your failures in life is the road to success.

The "Real Woman" is living in her new creation life on this earth enjoying the walk! Will the Real Woman please stand up!

Don't forget to stop and smell the roses.

About the Author

Joyce Tilney, founder of Women of God Ministries, teaching women today from women of yesterday, is a wife, mother and grandmother. Through her practical teaching and humor, women's lives are changed as they understand their role and identity as women of God.

Sharing personal experiences that impart hope and encouragement as she teaches the Word, many women are set free from the bondage of the enemy.

Joyce and her husband, Bill lived and ministered in Scotland for 12 years. During this time they pioneered two churches and Women of God Ministries was birthed. Traveling throughout Europe and Asia she knows and understands that the heart of a woman does not change from culture to culture or century to century.

Returning to the United States, the Lord spoke to her heart, "the printed word goes beyond your voice." For a season she published a Christian Newspaper. She has published several books and is a contributor to Charisma Online magazine and SpiritLed Woman.

She is a member of Harvest International Ministry under the leadership of Dr. Che Ahn.

Women of God Ministries

Recommended by Men of God

Dick Mills
Dick Mills Ministries

Psalm 68:11 in the Latin vulgate reads, "The Lord gave the Word of deliverance and the female evangelists who proclaimed it were a mighty host."

This verse is very applicable to Joyce Tilney and the anointed ladies making up the Women of God Ministries.

Betty and I have known Bill and Joyce Tilney and have been heart warmed by the work of grace in their lives. It's truly awesome to watch at close range the character development and the spiritual gifting and abilities God has given them both.

Joyce was given by the Lord a vision, a calling and an enablement to teach women the ways of the Lord. She has wisely followed the Lord in a very straightforward and disciplined walk. Her ministry is not a humanly structured program with a fleshly agenda on a calculated plan for building her empire. She is led by the Spirit, moving in the Spirit and anointed by the Spirit to impact women's lives.

One heartwarming facet of the Women of God is how easily her group fits in with all churches and denominations. She is equally at home with all church groups. Another facet that has impressed me is Joyce Tilney's ability to work with all women's groups that have invited her. She gets invitations from many women's organizations all over the world. She fits in easily with these groups because she is not clannish, doesn't have any feelings of elitism or exclusivity or territorial control.

I predict that this group and its sensitive and wise leadership will have a ripple effect that will reach to the ends of the earth to the end of the Church Age.

Edwin Louis Cole
Christian Men's Network
Bill and Joyce Tilney are true friends, and their ministry over the years has matured and now grown to international proportions. Biblically based and Christ centered, they present divine truth to be lived in practical life. Her Women of God conferences are excellent with lasting results. Bill and Joyce are two of God's choice servants and I recommend them without reservation.

Billy Joe Daugherty
Victory Christian Center, Tulsa, OK
Joyce Tilney is leading a special movement, Women of God Ministries. She was a faithful worker for Victory Christian Center when she and her husband lived in Tulsa, Oklahoma, USA. We rejoice for this hour that women are rising up to the works and spreading the Word of our Lord Jesus Christ.

Why Diets Don't Work
Food is not The Problem

This is not another diet plan, it is a battle plan!

We are in a crisis when it comes to our health and well-being-spiritually, emotionally and physically. You don't have to be a slave to your body and emotions. When I submitted my food addiction to the Lord, He gave me a battle plan that worked from the inside out and took 90 pounds from my body!

ALL BOOKS ARE AVAILABLE ON AMAZON

FOR MINISTRY DISCOUNT AND BULK ORDERS

PLEASE CONTACT: **therealwomanjt@yahoo.com**

Leah, the Substitute Bride
Rejected by Man, Chosen by God

Unsought, undesired and unloved- this was the story of Leah's life. She understood the pain of life. As she learned to cry out to God for help, she overcame the trials of life and fulfilled her purpose in life. Life is full of pain, but misery is optional for the Woman of God!

ALL BOOKS ARE AVAILABLE ON AMAZON
FOR MINISTRY DISCOUNT AND BULK ORDERS
PLEASE CONTACT: **therealwomanjt@yahoo.com**

Jochebed
A Mother's Decision that Saved a Nation

Most Christians don't even know who she is. The mother of three leaders; Moses, Miriam and Aaron. Her life speaks through her children. Listed in the "Heroes of Faith" (Hebrews 11), she was known by God. As a mother you have the opportunity to mold minds, nurture growth and develop potential like no one else!

ALL BOOKS ARE AVAILABLE ON AMAZON
FOR MINISTRY DISCOUNT AND BULK ORDERS
PLEASE CONTACT: **therealwomanjt@yahoo.com**

Fuel For the Fire
Man's Insecurities, the Devil's Security

Living a godly life in an ungodly world is not an easy assignment. Faith in God's Word offers us stability in life's every day journey and its unplanned detours. As we become established in the Word of God, abounding in thanksgiving, the enemies lies are exposed, and we overcome the insecurities in our lives that hold us in bondage.

ALL BOOKS ARE AVAILABLE ON AMAZON
FOR MINISTRY DISCOUNT AND BULK ORDERS
PLEASE CONTACT: **therealwomanjt@yahoo.com**